# Powered BY THE PIVOT

Secrets Revealed in My Journey Manifesting Peace, Love, and Gratitude

**CHERI WARCHOLAK LOHREY**

Powered by the Pivot:
Secrets Revealed in My Journey Manifesting Peace, Love, and Gratitude

Copyright © 2023. Cheri Warcholak Lohrey

All rights reserved. No part of this publication may be reproduced, distributed, or transmitted in any form or by any means, including photocopying, recording, or other electronic or mechanical methods, without the prior written permission of the publisher, except in the case of brief quotations embodied in critical reviews and certain other noncommercial uses permitted by copyright law. For permission requests, write to the publisher, addressed "Attention: Permissions Coordinator," at the address below.

ISBN: 979-8-9885147-4-9

Cover and Interior Design by Transcendent Publishing
www.transcendentpublishing.com

Author headshot and cover photo by Audrey Dempsey | Infinity Photos

*I have tried to recreate events, locales and conversations from my memories of them. To maintain their anonymity, in some instances I have changed the names and identifying characteristics of individuals, as well as the details of occupations and places of residence.*

Printed in the United States of America.

For my mother, Barbara Wade Warcholak.

# Contents

Author's Note .................................................................... vii

Prologue ............................................................................ ix

PART I: Pause ................................................................... 1

    Chapter One: Love ...................................................... 3

    Chapter Two: Nature ................................................... 7

    Chapter Three: Time ................................................. 23

    Chapter Four: Life, Death, and Diagnosis (2000 – 2010) ......... 35

PART II: Breathe ............................................................. 53

    Chapter Five: Be Present ........................................... 55

    Chapter Six: Facts .................................................... 59

    Chapter Seven: The Call ........................................... 69

    Chapter Eight: Believe .............................................. 81

    Chapter Nine: Standing ............................................ 93

    Chapter Ten: Scared ................................................. 99

PART III: Pivot .............................................................. 113

    Chapter Eleven: Unraveled ..................................... 115

    Chapter Twelve: Crushed ....................................... 119

    Chapter Thirteen: R.I.P. .......................................... 125

    Chapter Fourteen: Goodbye .................................... 131

    Chapter Fifteen: Alone ........................................... 133

    Chapter Sixteen: Interrogated ................................. 137

Chapter Seventeen: Shattered ................................................. 141

Chapter Eighteen: Escape ...................................................... 149

Chapter Nineteen: Action...................................................... 153

Epilogue ................................................................................... 159

About the Author ................................................................... 161

Acknowledgments.................................................................. 165

Appendix One: *"Powered by the Pivot"* Playlist............................ 171

Appendix Two: *"Powered by the Pivot"* Reading List .................. 179

Appendix Three: *"Powered by the Pivot"* Binge List ..................... 181

Appendix Four: Slogans and Quotes of Inspiration....................... 183

Appendix Five: Additional Resources............................................ 185

Thoughts of an Expectant Mother In 1973:................................. 187

Lessons Learned from our "Leaping" Leo................................... 189

Pause • Breathe •Pivot .............................................................. 191

# Author's Note

*Powered by the Pivot* is for everyone, to inspire growth and ignite action in your own life journey. It is for all friends that I have had the pleasure of meeting and friends I have yet to meet.

My dad always described me as the "social butterfly." I do wholeheartedly enjoy being social and gathering with people, be it in the United States or beyond, at a chance meeting on an elevator or in an airport, on Zoom or social media, or maybe in line for the bathroom. Everywhere we go is an opportunity to meet new friends – to learn, ask questions, discover something new, to laugh, to listen and to share. One of the best things I've been told about myself is "When you talk to people, you really listen."

This is for any and all people who support and listen to others, and especially for those who will be inspired to tell their story, share their voice, take action and pursue their dreams. Find a bit of solitude. Search your soul, set your goals, believe in yourself. Say it, Sing it, Shout it. Share your Story.

For anyone who brings joy, supports and empowers people, by encouraging others to Pause, Breathe and Pivot.

Always with Peace, Love, and Gratitude,

Cheri

# Prologue

For me, to pivot is to adopt an *I CAN Never Give Up* approach to life. It's a shift of mindset, an opportunity to discover Inner Peace, Strength, Love, and Gratitude when your plan for your life is unexpectedly shattered.

A gritty "type A," I was a planner, organizer, and social director with a plan and a *get-it-done* attitude. I was always in control, overcoming life's obstacles and dodging the curveballs… until I, along with my mom and sister, was run over by a "metal beast" of an automobile. This was most certainly *not* part of my plan, yet it's a headline in my life story, forcing me to Pivot in 1990.

I smile and giggle at other memories, stories shared, some of the precious moments in my life. I treasure them like the picnic basket that belonged to my mother. It holds their pictures and small tokens – a connection to my family that has passed on.

*Did I hear their stories? Did they share their voices?*

Merely seeing my ancestry basket reminds me of times when they, too, were here on Earth. It's a symbol of gratitude for touching my life. They are my soul, my roots, and have greatly influenced the person I am today.

Throughout this book, I randomly share a song that is on play in my mind. Maybe it's the title or the rhythm, or a feeling that touched my heart. I will reveal the full story, the raw facts of my life, but first, allow me to introduce myself.

I'm Cheri Warcholak Lohrey. I married my college sweetheart, Scott, twice (we renewed our vows on the beach for our twenty-fifth anniversary.) We are the parents of two incredible children – Alex, our firstborn, strong, handsome, driven, and mechanically-inclined son, and Aryn, our witty (and funny), determined, athletic, and beautiful daughter. We are also the parents of two fur babies, Cosmo and Leo, both standard poodles, yet so very different in personality. I'll explain later, but let's just say that nature does indeed make a difference.

As I'm awakened to write, the words pour out of me with the force of an avalanche thundering down a mountain. My story, it *must* be shared. It has marinated in my mind, been buried deep in my soul, for years.

*Hear my words. Listen to my voice. I do indeed have a voice.* My voice was left shaken and bewildered over thirty-two years ago when I was merely eighteen. How is this possible? How could time have passed so quickly? It has, and yet my heart still thumps, my tears still stream, and the lump constricts my throat as I relive that day in January when the blizzard rolled in. The day that changed the course of my life and undeniably forced me to *Pivot*. I travel back in my mind to deep, repressed memories, too painful to share until now. *I believe. I can.* This is therapeutic for *me*. This is *my story, my journey.* It's time for me to heal.

It has taken me over three decades to muster the courage to share my journey and discover my voice. As you read or listen to my story, my hope is for it to bring you joy, make you smile, and feel a sense of peace, love, and gratitude. Maybe, you will realize it's time for you to tell your own story. After all, we all have one worth sharing.

# PART I

# *Pause*

# Chapter One

## *Love*

### How Well Do You Sort Your Laundry?

My story begins in 1963, with a fortuitous connection at the laundry mat on an Army base in Aberdeen, Maryland. Yes, my parents' meeting was the result of my dad ending up with *pink* underwear. Here is how it unfolded (pun intended):

My father, Paul Warcholak, a handsome, fast-talking Jersey boy with an irresistible cleft in his chin, was stationed in Aberdeen as a member of the military police. Sharon, Mom's sister, was married to another MP, Bill Kisner, who was stationed at that same military base but worked a different shift from Paul. Sharon was the one behind the set-up and, ultimately, the reason I was born.

One day, Paul and Sharon were at adjacent machines in the laundromat. His load of whites nearly done, Paul opened the washer and was shocked to see that everything was pink – the result of a red sock accidentally tossed in. How had that damned red sock slipped in there undetected? Hearing Sharon giggle at his mistake, the Jersey boy laughed while shaking his head and uttering a few choice words under his breath, not realizing he was talking to his future sister-in-law.

This first contact led to future conversations in which Sharon and another young military wife named Faye played matchmaker. This was how you met potential suitors back then – the 1960s version of Match.com or eHarmony. Before they knew it, Sharon's sister Barbara was visiting from her home state of West Virginia to go on a blind date with Paul. Have you ever watched Alfred Hitchcock's *The Birds*? This was the movie Dad chose for their first date at the drive-in movies. *Frightening!*

My mom, Barbara Lynn Wade, was a kind, mild-mannered, and beautiful West Virginia girl. In 1965 at the age of twenty, she married my dad, age twenty-four. *Would my parents have ever met if my dad had successfully washed his whites on laundry day?* It's thought-provoking, but sometimes the smallest things can lead to the most incredible life changes.

### ♫ "Hey Paula" (Paul & Paula) ♫

My blond-haired, blue-eyed sister was born in 1968. Beth Ann was the apple of Dad's eye. He often called her "Sunshine," and she lived up to the nickname. Beth was an early riser and a chipper morning person.

A few years later, on a mild Virginia evening in the spring of 1971, my mom calmly washed her hair even though she knew she was in active labor.

Dad was on the golf course, and Mom, the considerate woman that she was, did not want to rush his game.

"Just let him finish his game," she insisted to the nervous neighborhood wives, "I'm fine."

When she retold the story years later, she casually explained that she had decided to *relax* at home. She took a bath, shaved her legs, and waited patiently for my dad to get home.

*Seriously? Active labor? His golf game? Interrupt him!*

By the time they were in the car headed to the hospital, Mom had become worried. Upon entering the hospital, she was placed on a wheeled hospital bed and whisked away to the delivery room, with

# 1 | LOVE

the nurses pleading with her, "Don't push! Don't push!" I arrived in this world at 12:33 a.m. on the one-year anniversary of Earth Day – my mom and dad's brown-eyed girl, with eyes just like my mom's.

Jon Paul, our blond-haired, blue-eyed, bouncing baby brother arrived in 1975. He completed our family until 1991 when Steffen joined our family on a foreign exchange program. My "other brother" from Germany lived with us for nearly a year.

> *Do you ever think, "I'm like my mom?" or "I'm just like my dad?"*
>
> *Do you recognize family traits in your kids?*
>
> *What molds us, our nature or nurture?*

## ♫ "Hip Hop Hooray" (Naughty by Nature) ♫

# Chapter Two
## *Nature*

**Old-School Style**

When I was little, we typically spent our school breaks visiting our grandparents in Florida. Road trips, like so many other things, were vastly different in the 1970s. There was no Waze or even MapQuest – Dad would drive with the paper map spread out across the steering wheel, his eyes darting between it and the road. The biggest challenge was folding that map back into its original form while he was driving.

For long road trips, Mom packed a cooler of sandwiches for the car; stopping for anything but gas seemed pointless to my father, who was focused on time. "Don't waste time," he'd often say, "We need to 'make good time.'" Dad kept a record of time and mileage on trips in a notebook in "line by line" detail. He even timed our bathroom breaks at the rest area. It was like we were contestants on the television show, *The Amazing Race.* He would stop the car and start his wristwatch – "Ready, go!"

On those longer trips, my siblings and I would claim our spots in the car. This was before seatbelt laws, and my older sister Beth would get to sleep and stretch out on the seat. As the middle child, I took the next-best spot, sunning myself by laying in the rear window sill – a cringeworthy thought today. Poor Jon was left with the hump on the floor, the woes of being the youngest.

## ♫ "Things that make you go Hmmmm" ♫
## (C+C Music Factory)

Let me tell you a bit about my grandparents, starting with Dad's mother, Anne Stasko, born on January 21, 1916. Originally settled in Brooklyn, New York, she later fell in love and moved to Paramus, New Jersey, where together with my grandpa, she raised her only child. Grandma was a meticulous housekeeper. Years later, in their retirement home in Florida, she wiped down the shower daily and, at times, she even scrubbed the driveway with bleach on her hands and knees. The way in which she cared for her belongings, she wasn't just going through the motions. She was teaching us about her story, her upbringing before arriving to the United States of America. Residing in the US during the Great Depression had clearly influenced her life, as well. Couches in their Florida home were covered with plastic. Yes, plastic. *Why did fitted plastic couch covers ever exist?*

While staying with them, my siblings and I slept in the den. Beth and I each got a twin bed that converted back into a couch by day, while poor Jon again got the short end of the stick: one of those plastic adjustable loungers that made the click, click, click sound as it opened. It would then be covered in towels, a sheet and blanket, and – ta-da! – he had a makeshift bed.

I recall early one morning, moseying down the ceramic-tiled hallway to the kitchen, squinting due to the bright Florida sunshine. When I got there, I found Grandma standing before her ironing board. Now, if you were to enter the kitchen, you'd see a smallish kitchen table with three avocado-green vinyl chairs immediately to your right. A fourth chair was positioned in a small cubby next to the refrigerator; above it, the phone was attached to the wall, its long cord spiraling down. There didn't appear to be room for one more thing, yet there in the middle of it, Grandma had managed to set up her ironing board. She ironed everything, including handkerchiefs – the ones you use to blow your

## 2 | NATURE

nose – and bedsheets. *I'm just waking up. How is Grandma almost done with a huge basket of ironing, and why is she ironing underwear?*

Grandma was a woman of small stature, petite, not even five feet tall. She was quiet and did not always have a lot to say, but there was a lot to learn from observing how she lived life. Dinners were always special – with fine china and proper table etiquette. I felt both special and nervous holding her fancy Mikasa cups and plates detailed with a delicate gold trim.

Grandma Warcholak was not only clean but tidy and wicked quick. She was known for making beds in the blink of an eye. If Grandma was visiting our home in West Virginia and she heard you get up in the morning, then you likely were not returning to bed.

Let me explain. If you got up to go to the bathroom – and depending on where Grandma was in the house – you had better tiptoe quietly back down the hallway to your room. Otherwise – and though you did not hear or see her, you'd get there to discover, to your horror, that the bed was made! No sign of Grandma except for a tidy room. Grandma lived by example. Our life together was worth celebrating, so she used her china. She also obviously lived by the notion, "the early bird gets the worm." There was no sleeping in while Grandma was in town.

My grandfather, though quite different in temperament, was her perfect match. Paul F. Warcholak, born April 6, 1916, was equally as hard working. He possessed a zest for life and a magnetic personality – you were drawn to him whether you knew him for twenty-two years or two minutes. And it didn't matter to him if you knew him as Grandpa, Grandpa Warcholak, Uncle Paul, or just plain Paul. "Call me whatever you like," he'd playfully say, "just don't call me late for dinner." He cracked jokes and wore a smile on his face that was contagious. Once per visit, Grandpa treated us to dinner at the buffet. He'd look at the sign taped to the cash register that read, "I need ones and fives," and say to the cashier, "You need ones and fives? Well, I need tens and twenties." Grandpa was always laughing at his own jokes.

Fast forward to my wedding day. Scott and I had chosen Julie London's rendition of "I'm in the Mood for Love" as our wedding dance, but the dance that would prove most memorable was my polka with my seventy-eight-year-old grandpa. This dance was not planned; it just flowed organically, with the entire dance floor lined with family and friends clapping to the music of the live polka band. It took me back to those childhood visits when we would put a vinyl polka album on the stereo, and Grandpa and I danced around the house together. One of our favorites was "Beer Barrel Polka" by Frankie Yankovic & His Yanks. My grandpa was certainly a "barrel of fun."

My grandpa possessed a loyalty and adoration for the love of his life, his wife, Anne, who passed away on May 30, 1993 at the age of seventy-seven. Ten years to the day of her death, Grandpa Warcholak passed away on May 30, 2003 at the age of eighty-seven. *Did he have that much control over the date of his own death?*

I treasure their memories with small tokens in my ancestry basket. I have Grandma's Estee Lauder Youth Dew Perfume and a small, delicate china shot glass to remind me of Grandpa. Grandpa's toast – "Over the lips and through the gums, look out stomach, here it comes" – was always delivered in his unique and lively fashion.

## Do You Believe in Love at First Sight?

I recently learned of my maternal grandparents' song: The Andrews Sisters' "(I'll Be With You In) Apple Blossom Time."

When Clara Ellen "Iris" Sleeth (b. June 26, 1918) first saw William Eugene "Jobey" Wade (b. April 28, 1917), she pointed him out to her friend, claiming, "That's the man I'm gonna marry." For my grandmother, it was a textbook case of love at first sight.

Everywhere Iris went, people would comment on how stunning her crystal-blue eyes were. Those who got to know her knew her heart was equally as beautiful. Her personality was the perfect combination of sweet and sassy.

What I remember most about Granny was how she made you feel. There was nothing better than sitting on Granny's lap to get a Granny hug. As she wrapped her arms around you, there was no doubt that you were safe, so special, and so loved.

Iris and Bill were the parents of three wonderful children: my Aunt Sharon, followed by my mom, Barbara, and their brother Billy. While the kids were growing up, they resided in Rock Lake on the outskirts of Fairmont, West Virginia. Rock Lake was a small, tight-knit community with cottages that surrounded the lake.

## A Pain in the Ass

One special memory of my grandparents is being at their house at Christmastime. We were all there: my parents and siblings and I, Uncle Bill and Aunt Sharon, and their three girls, Tricia, Amy, and Aly. As always, it was an adventure to drive out the winding country roads to Rock Lake. Once at the entrance, I remember sitting up in our car, wiping the condensation off of the windows so I could see the lake. I would certainly have to answer to my father later for leaving fingerprints *on the windows*.

As usual, we had driven around the lake, then crossed the small bridge and made a left turn down the lane to Granny and Pap Pap's cottage. Dad had barely pulled to a stop when my sister, brother, and I leaped out of the car. The burgundy-painted screen door made a creaking sound as it opened. A thin, dull metal coil stretched and then snapped the door shut. The screened-in porch was made from wooden planks that moved ever so slightly as we walked across them.

Upon entering their home, we saw the real pine Christmas tree, complete with silver tinsel, glowing in the corner. This was the tinsel that you would hand string, strand by strand, and larger colored bulbs strung across the branches. If you put your hand near the bulbs, you could feel the heat radiating from them, warning you not to touch. The air smelled of wood burning in the fireplace. Pap would be standing nearby with a black wrought iron poker in his hand, adding another log to the fire.

As he placed the next log on top, red sparks flew out of the fireplace. The sparks would turn to ash before they reached the floor. Hugs were given all around, then we would eat a homemade meal as we all crowded together in the small kitchen. The kitchen had white metal cabinets with silver pulls shaped like crescent moons. The drawers would squeak as they were opened and shut. Back in our day, there were two types of servings at "supper." You could have a regular serving or a "no, thank you" helping, which meant a smaller portion that you were still expected to eat. "Clean your plate" before being excused from the table was the rule.

With growing anticipation, we all would move into the family room together. I couldn't help but notice six boxes wrapped with ribbons lined up under the Christmas Tree. Once the gifts were distributed to the grandchildren, we waited for instructions from the adults on when we were allowed to open our present. The grandkids each received one gift from Granny and Pap Pap. *What could be in this cube-shaped box?*

Sounds of the ripping paper, then prying the lid open to look inside to see the one gift from my grandparents, one that I will always remember. My eyes widened, seeing the perfectly polished, brand-new white ice skates with shiny, silver blades that had *never* been used. All five of us girls got our very own white ice skates. *I would not have to wait for a hand-me-down.* Each pair had handmade colored yarn pom poms on them. Mine were purple and white pom poms, handmade with love by Granny.

*Where were we ice skating?* We were told to get our coats, hats, scarves, and mittens on and wait by the station wagon. According to the adults, we are all going together in the same car, *but how?* There were twelve of us. Pap got in the driver's seat of my aunt and uncle's station wagon. Mom and Aunt Sharon climbed in the middle row, and my dad and Uncle Bill put down the back gate. Our dads were all bundled up too, with their hats, coats, scarves, and gloves.

Any ideas on how they would take the six kids in the '70s? *Do you remember the wooden sleds with metal runners?* Well, my dad held the rope of a sled, and Uncle Bill held the rope of the other as they positioned themselves to sit on the back gate of the station wagon.

My sister was behind me, and I held my little brother in front of me on one sled. My three cousins were each in their colored one-piece belted and hooded snowsuits with coordinating winter boots on the other sled.

My dad and uncle casually chatted as they pulled us along on the sleds. It was dark at Rock Lake – no streetlights, just the moon and the stars and the headlights from the station wagon, which was pulling their precious children and grandchildren carefully.

When we reached the stop sign at the end of the lane, I watched the exhaust smoke billowing out from the tailpipe, we paused, and the red brake lights brightened. The only muffled sounds were from our dads' voices, the engine, and our sleds gliding through the snow making fresh tracks. I snuggled close to my siblings on our sleigh ride while our moms did not appear worried whatsoever. I remember seeing them smiling at each other – sisters gazing back at their kids and husbands, then turning to converse with their mom, our granny, who was in the front passenger seat. They all looked so carefree and blissful. This was indeed a lovely moment to remember.

Large white, fluffy snowflakes continued to fall ever so softly as they reached the tall evergreens with cascading branches that hung over the edges of the road. We were out in the country, where you could breathe; the air was crisp and clean. Dimly lit cottages surrounded the lake. I imagined what was happening inside the cottages; a game of cards near a fireplace, a man wearing a flannel and smoking a pipe while sitting in a wingback chair, or a grandma knitting, but always sharing some quiet conversation about their day.

When we arrived at the pavilion next to the lake, thoughts of summertime flooded my mind. In the summer, this is where we swam. Walking out into the water, feeling the bottom of the lake squish between your toes. We would have to work up the nerve to adventure out to the end of the pier.

At Rock Lake, the diving board was unusually high above the water due to the added height from the concrete pier. But the thrill that would get my heart pumping was the climb to the top of the slide.

This was not just any slide. This was a heavy-duty steel slide made to last, not for comfort. I recall feeling the connection of one metal piece of the slide to the next, the bump, bump bumps that were the uncomfortable ridges of friction against your *bum*, and occasionally a squeak which would be your skin against the dry metal if you did not happen to pump enough water when you were at the top.

There were no auto waterlines; we all pumped it ourselves with a hand pump. This meant you cranked the metal pump up and down repeatedly while standing high above the concrete pier, up in the air, at the very top of the gigantic, metal slide.

I was elementary school age. The breeze was blowing, my knees were knocking, the ladder beneath me filled with other kids, not so patiently, waiting their turn. I felt the pressure to quickly pump the water; I wished the water appeared faster. Being so high in the air at the top of the slide, my adrenaline was pumping. While standing at the top, the pressure to hurry was real. I had to pump enough water to wet the slide before sliding down. If I encountered a dry spot on the way down, I had no one to blame but myself. Once at the bottom of the slide, I was thrust off, only to collide with the water so many yards below. Even in the summer, the water was brisk. Swimming back to the pier and climbing up the ladder out of the dark water with a smile on my face. *I did it! Check.*

There was also a playground with swing sets that were exceptionally tall. I enjoyed swinging and then dragging my feet through the warm sand pits below. To swing, to feel the sun on my face and the breeze through my hair, was such a carefree summertime vibe that I loved.

But on this particular winter evening, we were shivering. There were bright orange and yellow flames erupting from the top of a metal garbage can with some fellow residents huddled around it, rubbing their hands together. The lake itself was frozen with a thick layer of ice and covered in a blanket of snow. Several men were clearing an area, shoveling the snow off the lake. *Why?*

The adults announce: We're here. *Wait, what? We are skating on the lake?* I'm feeling nervous again. We would use our brand new shiny white ice skates, complete with yarn-colored pom poms, and ice skate on Rock Lake. *Trust was the theme this holiday.*

## In a Puff

Pap Pap and his brother, Uncle Webbie, both packed their pipes with Sir Walter Riley stringy tobacco. The tobacco came in a can but Pap carried his tobacco in a soft, medium-brown leather, silver-zippered pouch. This was no regular zipper; it had an industrial thickness. Pap's pipe had a black staff and a brown, rounded, wooden chamber. He would strike a match. *Pause. Do you know the sound?*

I watched the flame from a match burn a brilliant bright yellowish orange, then dim as Pap hurried to light his pipe. Other times he would light it with a Zippo lighter with the flick, flick, flick of his thumb against the metal cylinder. This muted silver, original lighter was rectangular-shaped with an attached top that he would flip open in a single flick of his thumb.

Pap would inhale to light the tobacco with the flame by puffing on his pipe, then tilt his head back to blow circular smoke rings. He sat back, relaxed, and watched as he repeatedly blew smoke rings into the air. Smoking his pipe was a ritual beginning with sitting in his chair, leaning to one side to reach for the pouch in his back pocket, hearing the metal unzipping of the pouch, then watching him grab a pinch of the stringy tobacco and pack it in his pipe. This memory of sitting on the floor next to Pap as he prepared his smoke every afternoon is clearly captured in my mind, along with the distinct smell of smoke from his pipe. I sat close by and "zoned out" watching the smoke rings.

## Catch You on the Flipside

When Pap retired from Alcan Aluminum, my beloved grandparents moved to Florida full-time. Granny would go along with the relocation because it made Pap happy, but her heart, her family, and her home remained in West Virginia. Granny and Pap Pap kept in touch with family mostly through letters and recordings on cassette tapes they mailed back and forth. We would gather around a small cassette tape recorder and push play in order to hear their voices. Next, it was our turn to record and send it back to them. Back in the day, we actually looked forward to getting the mail. Staying connected was important

## 2 | NATURE

to our family. Occasionally Granny and Pap Pap called. At that time, you paid by the minute for your long-distance calls, so they were fewer and farther apart.

Let me tell you a little more about Pap. He was ambidextrous, which was handy in his softball days as both a lefty and a righty pitcher. He would take on any opponent – human, snake, or gator – be it at the horseshoe pits, on the pitcher's mound, or in the woods.

As the recipient of his pranks, you were never quite sure what pitch was coming your way. Pap enjoyed many hobbies, and one of his favorites was woodworking. While visiting their Florida home, our family helped lift an extremely tall birdhouse Pap had crafted. Granny loved birds. She had a large fountain for them in her front yard and a second birdbath closer to the house. Even though Pap made this lovely house for the birds outside, Granny and Pap also welcomed wild birds inside their home. What happened next? Pap grabbed the camera and started taking pictures of Granny with the wild birds perched on her elbow. It was like something out of the movies. Granny was just like Snow White – a retired edition, of course.

Pap Pap's woodworking talents were not limited to birdhouses. He combined his woodworking with storytelling when he created a rectangular wooden cage, probably twelve by eighteen inches in length and six to eight inches deep. This natural wooden box was affixed with chicken wire across the top and filled with hay so you could not see inside. On the top of the cage, written directly on the wood in bold red letters with permanent marker: *BEWARE: Dangerous Poisonous Hairy Lizard!*

Pap would lure you in as you listened to the tale of this rare reptile. You were scared but yet so very curious. Spectators were eager to catch a glimpse and be close to this dangerous creature, much like the anticipation while watching a horror movie, when you yell at the television for people to, *"Run!"* You know, when your rational mind tells you that nothing good is going to happen, but you do not move a muscle. Over and over, victim after victim would ignore their instincts. Pap sparked a curiosity that was irresistible. It's like the beginning of the song,

## ♫ "The Eye of the Tiger" (Survivor) ♫

Thump... Thump, thump, thump! It was your heart pounding in your chest, urging you to *run*. Many would do just that at the moment of impact, but it was too late. The poisonous hairy lizard would appear and smack victims squarely in the chest, leaving them terrified and gasping for breath.

Pap had made this whole contraption – the cage with the trip lever, the poisonous hairy lizard (sewn by hand) – spun a tale and brought the "caged animal" all the way from Florida when he visited. Pap could tell a story like no other. Times were different in those days. My grandparents did not rely on electronics; they were creative: telling stories, playing cards, singing songs, and playing jokes.

## Gag Me with a Spoon

One particular Thanksgiving, we were staying at my Granny and Pap Pap's house in Englewood, Florida. Granny would slip on the baby blue ruffled apron she had made herself over her head and tie it in a bow behind her back. She would prepare a meal, complete with delicious homemade pies that had finger-pinched crusts of perfection. Like many families, our Thanksgiving was a celebration of togetherness. My dad's parents were welcome to join us for our celebration at my mom's parents' house. *The more, the merrier.*

While waiting to be called by Granny, as she would say to *'*Go warsh up*"* for supper on that memorable Thanksgiving, we were all gathered in the living room with my parents, siblings, and paternal grandparents when my Pap came into the house. He looked down at his shoe and began to walk a little funny. Then Pap started to sniff.

"Do you smell something?" he questioned. We looked down at a brown-smeared glob, unsure what it was. "What is that??" Pap exclaimed. You stopped whatever you were doing to watch and listen to him. Then, practically, in slow motion (*Pap, what are you doing?!*), he put his finger in it and gagged. "Is that dog shit??? Did I really just step in dog shit?" A look of disgust appeared on his face as he brought his finger up to his nose, sniffing. Then, the worst part: in a slow strategic movement that everyone was watching, Pap actually licked his finger. "Yep, sure is!" Pap exclaimed. *Ewwww!!!!*

Totally grossed out, Grandma Warcholak began dry-heaving and quickly got up and hurried off to be sick in the *only* bathroom in the house. Pap cracked up, winked, and showed the rest of us that it was actually peanut butter. He had just added grass for the effect, Pap, the jokester.

I recall hearing the story of the alligator that was loose in their neighborhood. The citizens had called the sheriff's department to capture the gator. They did not get the response they wanted. *What do you mean, it's not your problem?!* Wrong thing to say to this tough group of older men. Pap, his brother Webbie, and a couple of his buddies were not taking "No" for an answer. They would capture the alligator, duct tape its mouth, and drop it off in the parking lot at the sheriff's office. "Well, Sheriff, now it IS your problem." Oh, brother.

We loved going to Granny and Pap's house. It was so welcoming and filled with life and with so much love. I learned it's important to stay connected to friends and family and have hobbies, as well as to be brave in my life.

Sadly, Pap Pap passed away on February 28, 1995, at the age of seventy-seven. Granny Wade passed on October 4, 1998 after her battle with Alzheimer's disease at the age of eighty.

I treasure my memories of my Granny and Pap Pap Wade with small tokens in my ancestry basket. I have a "mini" horseshoe to remind me of Pap. I wish I had his pipe. I have one of Granny's hand-sewn napkins, a handwritten Coconut Cream pie recipe, and a couple of her scarves that she wore. I also have pictures of them individually and as a couple in my basket. Their faces, their smiles, their love captured in old photos – priceless.

> *Pause and think about how life was different in those days. Think about your favorite memories with your grandparents. Write them down.*

My mom and dad taught me to listen to my gut, to get quiet and feel the feels, even the uncomfortable ones.

My dad modeled the importance of taking control of your own health with a focus on exercise. He often kept a detailed log of his workouts and would use his television time to do his at-home yoga practice. I learned to set goals, write them down, and check things off my list. He wanted me to be able to take care of myself, so he taught me to be independent. From an early age, I listened to him speak about the power of your thoughts. He really believed in these lessons and passed them on to me and my siblings.

My mom was a kind and gentle spirit who was welcoming and accepting of others. There was no doubt that she felt her most important job in life was to be a great wife and mother. She would tell me and my siblings that her job was not to do everything for us but instead to "teach us how to fly." She believed that things would happen in our lives for a reason. We may not understand it at the time, but we would surely have a lesson to learn. She lived a life choosing to look for the positive, even during tough times. When she was diagnosed with multiple sclerosis at the age of thirty-six, she would tell me that she was lucky. She had been able to enjoy her childhood and be an active mom when we were little. She lived with her MS with dignity and grace.

## Dig It

Growing up in the 1970s and 80s, I heard my parents often say, "Go play." We moved into Deerfield Estates when I was seven years old. My neighbor, Shelly Carvillano, lived right next door. Shelly and I quickly discovered we both liked to go, go, go. She was my roller skating, bike riding, hopscotch jumping, swimming, dirt digging, and cabin-building buddy. Additionally, we were tree climbing, sled-riding, and walking to the bus stop together with our neighbors.

As elementary school kids, we used to go into the "woods" behind our houses to dig our fort in the dirt with spoons. Then we would climb to the "tippy top" of the pines surrounding the cabin, probably ten to fifteen feet off the ground. We would enjoy standing at the very top of the trees, peering out high from our "lookout" over the entire neighborhood. While standing at the top of the tall pines, we would try to see how far we could sway the tree from side to side. It is really amazing that we did not catapult ourselves from the tree.

When our mothers hollered for us to come home, we would use our homemade "fire escape," as we called it. This meant holding onto a branch that would bend with your arms outstretched above you while hanging onto a branch above; then you'd release and drop about ten feet, through all the branches, to the ground. The branches were "fluffy" at the bottom, so we convinced ourselves it was a "cushioned landing."

Let me tell you, pine tree sap was a bitch to scrub off my skin, and our cushioned landing would leave us full of scratches and sap. Just imagine our parents taking one look at us, twigs and pine needles in our hair, questioning, "What the hell happened to you?" Those words would likely be from my dad or Shelly's mom. We could not sit at the dinner table the way we looked and smelled, like pine. "Where have you been? Go get cleaned up for supper."

Back in the '70s and '80s, telling your parents that you were bored would get you a *no, thank you* list of chores to complete. It was better to just disappear for the day. We just figured it out, even if it meant just lying in the grass in the front yard, staring at the clouds, and pointing out the cloud animals we imagined in the sky.

> *Pause: Take a break from your phone and connect with life. Step outside, put your feet in the grass, on the ground, in the sand. Pull back your toes and feel the blades of grass; feel the grit of the sand or dirt. Sit down, lie down, close your eyes. Just Breathe. Take time to be thankful for the I-cans in your life.*

# Chapter Three
# *Time*

**Oh, Snap**

During high school, I adopted the belief that I could be a model. *Why?* People would say, "You're tall, you're thin. You should be a model." I began to put pressure on myself to live up to certain ideals. As a teenager, I thought the models in magazines were naturally so perfect. I was clueless about airbrushing.

The process of getting photos began with a snap. "To snap a picture" was the sound the camera made when you captured the photo. In the 80s, you had to buy your camera and a roll of film – typically twelve, twenty-four, or thirty-six exposures. The number of exposures was how many pictures you could take. Once you had taken the pictures, you had to get them developed, which meant filling out the form, writing the check, mailing the film in… then waiting. When the envelope finally arrived in the mail, you would then examine the pictures to see that your eyes were closed or your head was cut off, only to start the whole process over again. My generation had to wait for everything.

My mom and I would evaluate the pictures to see if they were "modeling material," comparing them to girls in the magazines. I was five-ten and weighed a hundred and twenty-six pounds; I had a small dimple of cellulite on my outer thigh. I was already reducing my food consumption, so I did not know if this was possible for me to continue on this path.

The matter was settled by my dad, who became concerned about the restrictions I put on myself, and he put an end to it, abruptly. One weekend I was bent over the dishwasher unloading the dishes, and he grabbed the ass of my pants, snatched me right off the ground, and yelled, "You had better start eating!" This is just how "therapy" was done in my house. I would not go to counseling. Instead, I would heed the warning: just start eating or else! *Or else, what?* The full definition of what "or else" meant was not clear, nor did I intend to find out.

Life was just not easy for tall girls back in the eighties. My mom and Sue, our wonderful neighbor and her dear friend, told me, "Oh wait until you are older, you will love being tall." At that time, I was not convinced. In high school, I thought the shorter girls were so cute. They could wear clothes right off the rack at the mall, unlike my situation, where my ankles often were exposed before it was in style. I really wanted to "fit in" and to be fashionable.

In high school, I was involved in a lot of extracurricular activities. Like many, I preferred walking to class with friends. Shelly and I would walk together for a bit then separate as she entered the art room. I remember staring into the art room, wishing art was on my schedule too. I was drawn to the art room but, instead, I scheduled choir. We were told to pick either art or choir. I just accepted that I had to make a choice. I chose choir as my fine arts requirement. Period. I really should have been an advocate for myself. I'm not sure why I did not ask to take both. Opportunity lost.

## All That and a Bag of Chips

Fall 1989: I would live at home while commuting to Fairmont State College; after all, we lived in a college town. I helped out at home because my mom had MS. I was her legs for the grocery store, for errands, climbing up and down the stairs with laundry, et cetera. During my first semester of college, I pledged and joined a sorority as a legacy, following in my sister's footsteps. I had a case of F.O.M.O. (Fear of Missing Out). I had to satisfy my curiosity about sorority life, plus I loved staying busy.

Then, in January 1990, came "The Accident," the Pivot that changed the course of my life. I will share the details later, but for now, you need to know the rest of my story. I promise you will understand why by the end. This is the start of my love story that occurred as a result of changes in my life due to "the accident." My belief was that I am meant to be here and destined to follow a different path in life. *Why did I have to endure such a violent accident in order to Pivot?*

## My Homey: When I Realized My Best Guy Friend is No Longer Just a Friend

Meet Scott, my friend turned boyfriend and husband. This was the beginning of our love connection.

### ♫ "Just a Friend" (Mario) ♫

I met Scott during my sophomore year of college in the fall of 1990. He was a tight end on the football team recruited from Northeast Ohio. The following year I would learn that it was not an accident that I would see my "buddy" so often. Leah, one of my besties, would say, "One day, you are gonna end up in a lip-lock with him!"

Scott was the door guy at the college bar where my sorority sisters and I liked to dance. I still remember his strong "take charge" presence when he stood there, dressed in his gold-colored, work-issued sweatshirt, jeans, and high-top tennis shoes. Even though Scott and I were just friends, I enjoyed the extra attention from my football player buddy. He was tall and athletically built, with broad shoulders, dark hair, and big, green eyes. I would get lost in his eyes when Scott spoke to me, and his voice… I was delighted just hearing him say my name.

One night in the fall of 1991, the line to get in was long, so my friends and I decided we should take our big hair and trending outfits elsewhere. We were ready to head back to the car just as he saw me. Then Scott called my name. On that night, it was like a magnet was pulling me toward him. There was an undeniable connection. This would be the first night where I looked at him differently.

My eyes locked with his. Once I was within his reach, I noticed my heart beating faster in anticipation. As he opened his arms and pulled me close, he pressed his hand against the small of my back. Without another word, he leaned toward me; I felt the heat between us as he pressed his full, ribbon-shaped lips against mine. This was it, the first kiss, this moment of time, sealed in my mind.

From the moment he swept me into his arms, there were butterflies in my belly. I melted into him; it felt like no one else was around. It was cold outside, but heat rushed through my body; it felt nice to be in his arms.

As our lips parted, I told him, "I have to go with my sisters." He told me not to leave and took my hand, but my friends were almost in the car. I wasn't sure what had just happened, but I knew I liked it. As I pulled away, I smiled, leaving him wanting more. To my relief, my friends did not notice our brief interlude, so the questions would be delayed. This moment was on replay in my mind. I felt a strong bond with Scott already. This kiss would strengthen our friendship. Our relationship would never be the same, only better.

## ♫ "Get Outta My Dreams, Get Into My Car" ♫ (Billy Ocean)

The confession happened the following day as Leah was driving us to the Meadowbrook Mall in her dark blue Ford Escort hatchback. First, let me tell you about Leah's car. I thought she was one of the lucky ones – she had her own car! – but Leah was disappointed from the first moment she laid eyes on that little Escort. It lacked a certain love-at-first-sight appeal, in part because it was covered in what seemed like inches of dirt. When Leah saw her, she immediately gave her the name "Beastie."

What began with anticipation resulted in annoyance. Her "new for you" car that she was previously so excited to see had no power steering or power brakes, which made it a bitch to parallel park. Beastie also frustrated Leah with windows that fogged. To clear them, we would have to roll them up or down by rotating a little crank and knob.

It was a love-hate relationship with that little car. She got us safely to and from some fun times in college. The stories she could tell. Imagine a life with no social media to give away your secrets. Our conversations remain within our group and rest in peace with Beastie somewhere in an unknown junkyard.

Back to the confession. During our drive on 79 South, Leah had Beastie's heat on full-blast. "Leah, please turn it down. I can't breathe." The heat was continuously smacking me right in the face. I was like a dog trying to stretch her face up to the crack of the window for a little air. There was no temperature control in 1991. Leah liked the heat on high and the music loud. I am confident she was belting out some MC Hammer's "You Can't Touch This"; Vanilla Ice's "Ice, Ice Baby"; or Jodi Watley's "Real Love" from her cassette tape collection.

I was working up the nerve to divulge, hating to admit she was right. I start to recap what *may* have occurred at the door of the bar last night. As I disclosed the first kiss, "Na, uh." Pleasantly surprised, she immediately turned down the music and banged her palm on the steering wheel, all while smiling, laughing, and saying, "Scott's so good for you."

Meanwhile, at my parents' house, I had missed a call. Here was how it worked when I was in college: you had to be home to get a phone call. No phone or internet at your fingertips; when I returned home from shopping, Mom just said that a guy with a really nice voice called but did not leave a message. *Who was the guy with the nice voice?* Phone calls in the '80s and '90s no doubt would result in your family being guests of your conversation. There was no real privacy. You were stuck by the length of the phone cord, talking in front of whoever was in the room.

I was twenty and Scott was twenty-one when we began dating. He was a big, "tough" football player. I wanted him to know that I was "tough" too and could take care of myself like my parents had taught me. Scott had arrived at my parents' house one evening when Dad and I were rotating the tires on our car. Scott wanted to take over and lift the tire to help me. I refused, pushing past him with a bit of an attitude. "*I can do it!*" I enjoyed knowing I could take care of myself. At the same time, it was nice to have my man around to spoil me. We grew stronger as a couple but also respected each other as individuals.

After his graduation, Scott returned to Ohio for a job in his career field while I finished college. We continued our long-distance relationship. Scott and I were engaged on June 9, 1993, my mom's birthday, at Valley Falls State Park in West Virginia. While we were apart, I concentrated on finishing school, student teaching, and planning our wedding.

## ♪ "Anytime" (Brian McKnight) ♪

## As If

My parents said, "If you want us to pay for the wedding, then you will not live together first." Period, no discussion. Fortunately, I married my soulmate, Scott, on July 30, 1994.

# 3 | TIME

Following our wedding and reception, we drove to Pittsburgh for our honeymoon night since we had an eight o'clock flight to Orlando the next morning. *Seriously, why so early?* I am just *not* a morning person. The next day, in my usual fashion, I was running late to get to the airport. My 1990 maroon Ford Probe five-speed was still covered in the shoe polish the bridal party had used to decorate it. There was no time to wash the car before we left it to bake in the parking lot of the Pittsburgh International Airport.

Scott was speeding to make the flight, and before we knew it, we saw flashing lights as a cop raced up behind us. Pull over! Scott stopped, and the officer approached, asking for license and registration. Obviously noticing the "Just Married" decor all over the car. He asks Scott specifically where we are going. Spoiler Alert: Scott was trying to make our honeymoon destination a surprise. *Apparently, we are going on a cruise to the Bahamas. Check.*

While we waited, Scott turned to me and said, "I'm sorry, that is not the way I planned for you to find out." I was happy to be married to a planner. He understands me. In our relationship, I am typically the idea person equipped with lists, planning, and organizing around the house. He is the "idea" person when it comes to travel, entertainment, and moving. Scott takes action. When he is talking about it, the plan is likely in motion. He is a "why wait?" kind of guy, and that time my "driven man" got off with a warning.

We were literally running late, running like fools through the airport to catch our plane. We were so late that the flight attendants had already given up our seats for Scott's first flight ever. We did get to Orlando, but when the last suitcases came off the conveyor belt, ours were missing. We waited in line at the baggage claim to find out what happened. They said that we had "voluntarily separated" from our bags. We had done no such thing! Well, when you arrive at the gate ten minutes before the plane departs, you automatically agree to separate from your bags. "Your bags will be arriving on the ten-a.m. flight." *I wish I was scheduled for the ten-a.m. flight too!*

Our honeymoon cruise was memorable, with sunshine glistening over the turquoise blue waters. Even though our ship was gigantic, I was a little nauseous and off-balance all week. After the cruise, we were scheduled for a few more days in Orlando. Upon arrival at the hotel, we decided to take a dip in the pool. The pool area was lovely and had a tropical vibe, complete with palm trees and reggae music. Ladies in braids from the cruise were at the pool; couples were in "chill-out" mode. I sat on the deep side of the pool, then lowered myself into the warm water, beginning with my toes all the way up to my shoulders. "The water feels great," I said to Scott. Still disoriented, in mid-air, he couldn't decide whether to jump or dive in. So he did a combination, with his lower body jumping in feet first and his upper body, including his arms and face, in proper form to dive. *Wait, what is he doing? Bad idea, Honey, abort!*

In life, indecision may get you smacked in the face, which is exactly what happened to my groom. His face and his arms smacked the water with such force sending a splash and a ripple traveling throughout the pool. We started laughing. I am still giggling. *I adore my man.* My husband has taught me to never be afraid to make an entrance.

## ♫ "Three Little Birds" (Bob Marley) ♫

## Let's Bounce

Our next stop would be my parents' house. Scott had been sleeping in so many different locations over the past week and a half. He traveled from our home in Painesville, Ohio, to the hotel in West Virginia for a couple of days before our wedding, next to Pittsburgh before our flight, then the cabin on the cruise ship, and so on. Now Scott and I would sleep in my childhood room, the room I had slept in since the age of seven.

The walls were painted a pepto-bismol-colored pink. I smile, reminiscing about Grandpa Warcholak standing on a ladder painting my room wearing his painter's cap, cut-off belted shorts, and his light blue button-up sleeveless painter's shirt with frayed edges. He was smiling with the paint roller in his hand and speckles of pink paint all over his face.

Tired from a long day of travel, Scott and I headed to bed. In the middle of the night, Scott sat up abruptly. He jumped out of bed and began searching for something in our suitcases, but what was he looking for? My sleep was interrupted by the noise.

"Honey?" I asked. "What are you doing?"

"We've got to get off the boat!" he said in a panicked voice, "We've got to get off the boat!" Clearly, this was an emergency. Scott continued searching through our suitcases. Forgetting where I was, I sat up, concerned that I could not get off the ship the way I was.

"Oh my God! Get me my bathing suit! Get my bathing suit top! Honey, I need my bathing suit top!" If the ship was really going down, I knew my man would make sure I got what I needed.

We never did figure out what he was trying to find in our suitcases, but the next morning I woke up clutching my bra. *Ha, too funny!*

Later that night, we all visited with family and friends around the dining room table at my parents' house. We enjoyed Mom's delicious, homemade pizza. I was saying so long to my childhood home and putting my memories away for a rainy day. Our neighborhood was a great place to grow up, and throughout our town people were friendly, smiling and greeting you even if you did not know them personally.

## Booyah
## Newlyweds- July 1994 - 1999

My first full-time teaching position was teaching fourth grade for Painesville City Schools in Ohio. I was looking forward to our life together and starting a family, but my goal was to complete my Master's in School Counseling before getting pregnant. I applied for graduate school right after I accepted my first job and soon received an acceptance letter from Kent State University Graduate School. *Check.* Earning my master's degree before having kids was part of my plan. My handwritten datebook was my lifeline. I would fill up the daily blocks in my calendar and then check them off. This was so satisfying for a checklist person like me.

My daily checklist looked something like this:

- 5 a.m.: Alarm goes off

- 6 a.m.: Teach spinning class at YMCA every Mon, Wed, and Friday.

- 7 a.m.: Depart from the YMCA

- 7:15 a.m.: Arrive home, get ready for work

- 8:30 a.m. - 3:30 p.m.: Teach 4th grade

- 4:30 - 5:45 p.m.: Commute to Kent State University (once or twice a week)

- 6 – 9 p.m.: Graduate school classes

Other evenings were designated for lesson planning, grading papers, researching and completing projects for graduate school, date nights, and our social life. My schedule during the school year was on repeat. I focused and planned just about everything for my day-to-day schedule, from lunches to outfits all the way down to my undergarments. I was focused on efficiency, yet I did not understand the need for cell phones.

At work, there were no phones in the classrooms and no voicemail; this was before internet and e-mail. Instead, I would retrieve handwritten messages from my "mailbox" – a little open wooden slot labeled "Mrs. Lohrey" located in the school's main office. One day I had a handwritten message on a little pink piece of paper that read, "Call Scott in his office."

I had to walk down the hallway to the teachers' lounge to use one of the two phones available in the school for teachers. I dialed his office number. Scott answered and got right to the point. "What do you think about getting cell phones?" *Really, why? I don't know what I would use it for.* Yes, it's true, those were my thoughts about cell phones in the '90s. It seemed like a waste of money to pay for cell phones. *What would I do with a cell phone?*

I graduated from Kent State University with a Master's in School Counseling. A couple of months later, I accepted my first School Counseling Position at Memorial Junior High School with the South Euclid - Lyndhurst City Schools, starting fall of 1999. I would adjust to teaching my spinning class time from six a.m. three times per week to six p.m. once a week.

Then, one morning in September 1999, I had a positive pregnancy test. I was flying to Virginia that day to be with my cousin, Amie Warcholak (soon-to-be Mrs. Amie Francis), for her bachelorette party and bridal shower weekend. Since it was Amie's special weekend and too early to be making any announcements, I was not ready to share the news of my pregnancy.

I volunteered to be the designated driver. As DD, I would avoid questions about having a cocktail during the celebration.

Great News: My mom and dad moved from West Virginia to Ohio near our home. Life was happening according to plan. I was a busy pregnant wife, school counselor, spinning instructor, planner, shopper, organizer, daughter, sister, aunt, friend, and bridesmaid. With my parents within closer proximity, I could visit regularly with them after work. Especially with my mom's MS progressing, it was so nice to see her more often. With her in town, I could assist more frequently instead of planning weekend trips to West Virginia.

# Chapter Four
# Life, Death, and Diagnosis
## (2000 – 2010)

**Sucky**

My mom continued to manage her MS. Unfortunately, Dad also began dealing with some unsettling symptoms, which led to the discovery of his Parkinson's Disease. Reflecting on this, I am reminded that life does not always happen according to plan.

**Sweet**

Throughout the school year, I continued my busy schedule – working full-time, preparing for the arrival of our first baby, teaching spinning weekly, and visiting my parents regularly. By May 2000, I was very pregnant, and my due date was within a few weeks. My OBGYN told me the baby was currently breech; she also insisted that it was time for me to get off the bike and stop teaching spinning class. There was still time, and the baby may flip. Thankfully, the baby did flip into the proper position. I remember walking lap after lap around the maternity floor halls while my husband watched the Cleveland Indians baseball game on television in the birthing suite. Later, I pushed for fifteen minutes to give birth to our little "slugger." It's a boy! Since we planned on having kids, I already knew our son's name even before I was pregnant with him. Alexander was a family name, my grandpa's father's name. We welcomed our blond-haired, blue-eyed baby boy into our lives. Alexander Scott had arrived, and my world forever changed.

My life working in the schools provided me with extra time in the summer months to bond with my baby. In August, I returned to work, which was heartbreaking. For me, the intense instinct to watch our son, to cuddle him and be near him, was real. We continued our family plan. Our life together was on schedule. Now I was a mom, wife, daughter, daughter-in-law, sister, aunt, sister-in-law, friend, school counselor, spinning instructor, and… we're pregnant again! Baby #2, coming spring of 2002. The second pregnancy just felt different, more intense, more exhausting. Scott would often tell me, "You better hope that's a girl in there." It was his turn to name our baby, and he decided on Aaron for a boy and Erin for a girl.

It's a girl! *Check.* Our daughter A-R-Y-N Mackenzie Lohrey was born at the end of March. (Scott agreed to let me choose the spelling.) When we got home from the hospital, new schedules and routines were starting to take shape. Everything was great, until…

By June, my mom had started vomiting almost continuously. She was losing weight. I could see her collarbone protruding from her neckline. As the school year came to an end, my sister Beth and her kids, Zach, Andrew, and James were arriving from Martinsburg, West Virginia, to Mom's house in Ohio for a visit. With Beth's added persuasion, Mom finally agreed to go to the Emergency Room. The hospital admitted her and scheduled a biopsy, which revealed ovarian cancer that had already spread throughout her entire body. Everything was happening so quickly.

My head was spinning while trying to care for my two young babies. My mom was brave and chose to come home to Valleyview Drive in Painesville, Ohio, with hospice care. Thankfully, my Aunt Sharon and my cousin Tricia who was studying to be a nurse came to help. Their presence and care for Mom was incredible and so very appreciated. Within weeks of the initial diagnosis from the biopsy, my mom was having her last moments. She read *Bears on Wheels* to her grandson, Alex, age two. She put her arms around her baby granddaughter, Aryn, and cuddled with her one last time.

The last food item she asked for was a root beer float. A quick trip to Dairy Queen, she took a couple of sips and then closed her eyes. On July 6, 2002, just three weeks after we learned of her diagnosis, Mom passed away peacefully in her sleep in the middle of the night with my dad at her bedside. We had lost my mother, our precious loved one – wife, mother, grandmother, aunt, and friend – at the young age of fifty-seven. She was gone way too soon, leaving me heartbroken with an undeniable emptiness in my soul.

There are so many beautiful ways to describe my mother: kind-hearted and compassionate, a beautiful friend, a saintly woman, a spirit like no other. I am grateful to be her daughter.

Her gravestone reads:

### Barbara L. Wade Warcholak

### June 9, 1945 - July 6, 2002

*"Her friendship was an inspiration, her love a blessing."*

I was thankful to be on maternity leave and have extended time off due to the summer. As I returned to work in August, I quickly hustled through the main office area with my head down, trying not to make eye contact with anyone. Then Principal Tim Jarvie walked down "The Doris Govan Guidance Wing" of the office of Memorial Jr. High School and welcomed me back with a big smile and a warm, "Hi!

You're here! His voice was so upbeat and happy to see me. "Oh... you're crying." Within minutes of my arrival, it was time for tissues. Separating from my baby girl and my two-year-old son was heart-wrenching, magnified by the loss of my loving mother over the summer. It was a rough start to the school year. Thankfully my colleagues at Memorial Junior High were more than just co-workers. We were a "work family."

In the summer of 2004, I was invited by my dear friend Shari to register for the MS Pedal to the Point. This charity event held for research of multiple sclerosis was a way for me to honor the life of my mother. Shari, who I had met in our school counseling program at Kent State University in the late 90s. We were known as "the Sharis" or "the Cheris," as we often scheduled classes together, along with our friend Kim.

Kim was from the west side of Cleveland, Shari from the southeast, and I from the east side in the snow-belt. The three of us met and bonded. Kim and I had a longer commute, so we would often get books on disc from the library and listen in the car, like our own little book club. I looked forward to connecting with my grad school friends during graduate school and beyond.

Now, still wanting to do everything with two small kids at home, there was no time to train by road cycling. I trained for the MS charity event by indoor cycling in our home. Shari and I would cycle together at the Berea Fairgrounds in Cuyahoga County on the first day of the event, bike seventy-five miles, and then shower at Sandusky High School.

After a challenging day of cycling (*seventy-five miles, check*), Shari and I, along with a group of other hot and sweaty, naked women, stood in the communal shower area of Sandusky High's girls' locker room. Not glamorous at all, but there's no way you can skip a shower after cycling seventy-five miles! After dinner, we set up for sleep in the hot, stuffy gymnasium. Our reward for cycling all day was a complimentary ticket to go to Cedar Point's Amusement Park, Sandusky, Ohio. *Um, thanks but no thank you.*

On day two, we would need to bike the seventy-five miles back. *Ouch! Oh, my goodnesssssss!!!!!* Let's just be real, the ouch was the bike seat that was *not* so forgiving on the "who-ha" on day two. *Yikes!*

My legs were sore, my body fatigued. Is this how my mother felt with symptoms of MS? I focused on cycling, one push of the pedal, one pull of the pedal, one stroke at a time, thinking of my mom. I zoned out imagining her daily challenges, thinking, *I can* do this for her.

## ♪ "Mom" (Meghan Trainor) ♪

My father, Paul Warcholak, was not the easiest person to live with during my childhood, but I truly have learned so much from him. I learned that things in life are not given, they are earned. As a result, I learned to be a hard worker. I learned that in order to reach your goals, you should have a plan. Therefore, I have goals and write them down. He emphasized the importance of self-care and exercise. I have learned to get quiet, listen to my inner voice, be still, and trust myself. *Thank you, Dad.*

After my mom passed, Dad's Parkinson's disease was more evident.

Allow me to paint a picture of my father – his love, his support, and dedication to family – in one story. In 2008, when Aryn was just six years old, my father was feeling ill and needed to go to the hospital. Aryn was participating in an organized recreational soccer game. He insisted that we go to Aryn's soccer game to support his granddaughter before going to the emergency room. He was unable to sit as a regular spectator on the sidelines, so he directed me to drive my car down a service exit to get closer to the field. My dad was in so much pain that he could not fully stand up, so he leaned over his walker. After the final whistle blew, he said she did such a good job. *How did he know since he could not fully lift his head to see the game?* He said, "I know because I could hear everyone cheering for her." He was so proud. This once lively man would never attend another sporting event. *I'm all choked up. Pause. Breathe.*

In the fall of 2008, he would be admitted to the hospital and then relocated to the nursing home. On the day he passed, I was sitting at his bedside, sharing old photos and reminiscing with him about stories of our family. Hours passed without any communication from my father. The hospice nurses would assess his vitals regularly and finally asked me to take a break. His heart rate was registering in a manner that they felt he did not want to pass away in front of me. My father did like to control situations in our house, so I was not surprised that he wanted to pass on his own terms.

It felt surreal as I hugged and kissed my father, saying goodbye in disbelief that this was happening. As the nurses suspected, my father soon passed. I received a call about fifteen minutes after I left his room. My father was sixty-seven years young when he passed away. My dad would leave the body that had burdened him to join my mother, his soulmate. My father's love for my mother can best be described by the quote he chose on their shared gravestone. It reads:

### Paul V. Warcholak

### Born September 8, 1941 - November 17, 2008

*"I've loved another with all my heart and soul,*

*and to me, this has always been enough."*

This quote really says it all. *Pause. Breathe.*

# 4 | LIFE, DEATH, AND DIAGNOSIS

> *Do you visit cemeteries where your loved ones are buried?*
>
> *Do you have conversations about life? About death?*

## My Peeps

In the spring of 2009, I had a great idea. I would sign up for the Fairport Harbor Pirate Triathlon as a tribute to my dad, who was dedicated to health and fitness. When we were younger, he would make us kids go with him on walks. He would use his stopwatch to keep track and log both the time and distance on his calendar.

I somehow convinced a few friends from work to train with me for the Pirate Triathlon Sprint event scheduled for July 2009. The triathlon sprint consisted of a .5-mile swim (750m), a 12.4-mile bike (20k), and ending with a 3.1-mile run (5k). Ericka Blackburn, Kelly Puhalsky, Cathy Valaitis and I decided to register. Some of us took fitness classes at the Central YMCA, and Cathy was the physical education teacher at LaMuth Middle School in Concord Township, Ohio, where we worked together, but I would not have considered any of us competitive athletes at this point in our lives. We were co-workers, moms, wives, sisters, and friends. Gratitude for my friends who stick by me and do the hard things to show their support.

The race began and ended in Fairport Harbor, Lake County, Ohio. Fairport Harbor is a coastal town on Lake Erie. This small village was a "fisherman's treasure."

In July 2009, I felt positive. *We Can Do This.* My dad would have advised, "Pace yourself," so I did just that. I was pacing myself for completion. The four of us were ready with our hair in ponytails, bathing suits, and goggles; our bikes were prearranged, waiting in rows just off the beach. *Check.*

In the early morning, the water was refreshing as we walked out into the lake through the waves. The mass of thirty-five-plus-year-old women was all crowded together, attempting to maintain our starting positions. At five-ten, I was able to stand flat-footed out in the lake. Attempting to stay together, my friend Ericka was hanging onto me. All stretched out at five feet tall, the water at the starting point was already over her head. The race gun fired, and within seconds my friends were unrecognizable. Arms, feet, and splashing water everywhere. *It's time, start swimming. Fifty-meter* (.5 miles) *swim. Check.*

At the conclusion of the swim, it was tough running from the water's edge through the sand. I had a small bucket of water and a towel set up next to my bike and was attempting to remove as much sand as possible so I could put on my shoes and hop on my bike. My friends' bikes were still there. Time for me to keep moving. Today, a very doable 20k/12.1-mile bike ride on the checklist.

I heard my father's words in my head. "*Cheri, just pace yourself.*"

I got on my bike, a 1994 Cross Trainer, which was not a competition bike but allowed me to be in the race. Push forward around the gear, then pull up on the backside using the cage surrounding my feet. I continued that push and pull within the pack of fellow triathletes. My muscles engaged quads, hamstrings, and calf muscles all pedaling synergistically — 12.1 miles on the bike. *Check.*

My legs felt like jelly as I dismounted the bike. My quads were burning, my hamstrings were tight, and a heaviness weighed down my body. I shrugged it off as expected from swimming and cycling back-to-back. I began my self-talk. I saw my hubby and the faces of my sweet daughter and son in the crowd on the hill. Their support was motivation to push a little harder.

After the initial climb, the remainder of the run was fairly flat, although the sensation I was experiencing was like there was tar on the bottom of my shoes. It was challenging to lift my feet; my pace felt slow. Once I passed the three-mile marker, I knew I was almost there. I heard someone coming. *Oh Crap, I'm being passed.* It's my friend, Cathy, smiling and waving. "You doin' okay?" she asked, smiling as she passed me. I said, "*Yes,*" smiling, trying to ignore the heaviness in my body. I looked around, thankful no one else was approaching.

Then, unexpectedly, the left side of my body locked up, namely my left leg. *Wait, what the hell is happening?* As if it happened in slow motion, my left foot did not quite pick up, my shoe scuffed the concrete, and I was thrust forward against the warm, rough roadside, with only my hands preventing me from falling completely on my face. As I looked up, I felt the sunshine. The final stretch is near. *C'mon, get it together Cher, you can do it, keep going.*

My dad always taught me to set my goals, make a plan, and just do it.

Next, I pushed off the pavement with a little grunt, looking around to see if anyone heard or saw me. I walked for a little bit, then began to jog as I rounded the corner for the final stretch lined with people standing behind the triangular, colored flagged ropes. I felt puzzled as I saw the man working the race coming toward me, followed by my husband and my kids. *What did I look like?* I began feeling paranoid. *What was wrong with me?* 3.1 mile-run. *Check.*

The following week, recapping with my friends at work, I remember being told by my sweet friend Kelly that her mom, Sylvia, was concerned about me. "There's something wrong with Cheri!" she had told Kelly several times. I'm not sure what occurred during the race. As a result, I scheduled an appointment with my doctor, which would become a regular neurologist appointment over the next year.

## ♫ "Dazed & Confused" ♫
## (Jake Miller, featuring Travie McCoy)

## July 2009 - August 2010

I felt small, insignificant as I arrived for my neurologist appointment, a referral to the Mellon Center in Cleveland, Ohio. The entrance was filled with huge windows on this cloudy, overcast day. It was a depressing and discouraging environment, synonymous with the current theme in my life. Just over a year ago, I was training for the triathlon sprint and running three to five miles a day. I told myself, *I am fine. I don't belong here*, but I recalled my struggle while training for the triathlon. One morning when I was running on the treadmill before work, I tripped and fell. I must have sensed that something was wrong because I was wearing the emergency stop cord. I fell and hit the treadmill with such a force. "BAM!" Let's just say that fall made such a loud, startling sound that Scott came rushing in from the other room. I giggled because I was not hurt, but the treadmill, not so much. The platform had completely collapsed into two pieces, and I left black tread marks on the wall from my shoes. Oops!

While waiting for my appointment, I observed others struggle with a compromised gait using a cane, a walker, or a wheelchair, not even walking at all. This was what was being shown to me. It was like it was being announced over the intercom. *Uh hum, please pardon this interruption, Cheri Warcholak Lohrey.* It sounded something like this in my head, "*Cheri Lohrey, here is your dreary future, walking with a compromised gait or not walking at all.*" This place was intended as a place to help me heal; instead, it just put me in a funky mindset. As a result, I began a self-fulfilling prophecy. I began to lose weight and dress like I was ill. After all, my future was looking pretty dismal.

Diagnosis day was like a ride down a deep, dark, scary lane. The denial was real and often hidden behind timid grins. My life was now filled with unknown twists and turns that would have me stumble during the day and go bump, likely into a wall, at night. The challenges eerily crept into my body and settled onto my soul. It felt like a ship entering a thick fog of unsettling waters, unsure of what lies ahead.

Everyone was "so sorry" and tried to assure me that it would be alright, but it doesn't feel that way when you are losing control of your body and, quite possibly, your mind. The sad reality of my day-to-day, hour-by-hour abilities was looming in life's unknowns; they were all so unpredictable. *What was anyone supposed to say upon learning of my diagnosis?* I know friends meant well when they said, "I'm sorry," but no response would sound reassuring. It's the reaction. The fear, the looks of sorrow and concern of friends and family who were all thinking of the same frightening and concerning thoughts I was. Will she walk? For how long? When will she be in the wheelchair? *Listen, I got it, I am concerned and wondering too.*

Larry David, the writer of Seinfeld, just may have the right idea, as revealed in an episode when Jerry and Elaine were waiting for their friends David and Beth's marriage to crumble. The line "I'm here for you" is actually the most comforting. With so many losses associated with MS, I really wanted to know that my friends and family would be there. I understand the "out of sight, out of mind" that happens naturally. I desire to continue to fit in with my friends' lives. MS becomes an increasingly lonely existence. The reality is that I have limitations on the length of participation due to intense fatigue that can occur unexpectedly. I am forced to face my personal nightmare, accept the facts that suck, and figure it out.

The "looks"; I analyzed the looks. My mindset got darker. The more I thought, the more I learned, the more I felt I didn't really know. I read. I listened. I pondered. My head was spinning. Well, maybe this and maybe that, but no one ever really knows with any certainty. The frequency with which I reached out to friends decreased. My once physically active life that I knew and loved, I just didn't have the energy to do anymore. *Losing my balance, losing my mind, losing my body, it is all just too much. Please make it stop.* I needed to quit thinking and talking about the MS, the decision, and the indecision.

"What treatment are you going to do??? What are you doing? What are you doing? What are you doing?" Stuck on repeat. The questions were plentiful, but where were the answers? The real answers that actually work? I read about the toxins, the side effects, and the possible negative outcomes. I felt like my life was not my own, a research study of what may happen. *Well, we are not really sure.* I read more, called nurses, talked to doctors, asked questions, inquired about clinical trials, and became more confused. Everyone had an idea, but the ending was always the same. I would think I knew what I would try, only to be hit with more of the same ending statement. *Well, we don't really know for sure. Everyone is different.*

I became frustrated and confused all over again. My husband was my sounding board through it all. The poor guy sometimes just did not know what to say. I was trying to find a balance between talking about it and not talking about it. I did not want to deal with this. I had things to do. I wanted to do what was best for me and my family. When I was asked how I was feeling, I just did not know. *All I know is that I'm not sure of anything anymore.* I felt like the lyrics written by Tori Kurtz in "Hurricane" (Willingness):

> *Heavy rain*
> *Violent storm*
> *Let it drain out*
> *Let it pour*
> *Ocean Tide*
> *Pull me in*
> *Let it carry me*
> *Again*
>
> *Oooh*
> *Oooh*
> *Ooooh*
> *I can barely breathe*
> *Underwater..."*
> *How can I*
> *Free my mind*

## 4 | LIFE, DEATH, AND DIAGNOSIS

…The mind games of my MS diagnosis began to sink in.

The entire diagnosis process from 2009 to 2010 involved a lot of poking, prodding, and pin testing (yes, the testing was poking me repeatedly with pins, appointment after appointment). *Please stop poking me!*

The doctor would ask, "How does this feel? Sharp or Dull?" Both responses annoyed me. I mean, who really enjoys being poked and then asked to evaluate the sharpness of how the poking feels? Your heart starts to race, afraid that you did not feel something. My awareness was heightened to the feelings, or rather the lack of feeling, the reaction or lack of reactions, made by my body.

One that rocked my world was when my doctor asked, "With your feet on the floor, can you lift your big toe on your left foot?" *Wait, what?* Initially, I thought, *No problem,* and then I looked down; damn it, lift already. *What the hell? My freaking toe… hello, pick up.* I gulped. There was a lump in my throat. I wished my big toe would just lift already. The struggle to control the tiniest parts of my body became my reality. After this appointment, I started practicing moving my big toe. *Like, seriously, how did I go from training for a triathlon to trying to lift my big toe?*

Then lastly, an MRI and spinal tap, which provided the confirmation of the multiple sclerosis diagnosis, the MS. By the way, you sign away your rights when you get your spinal tap. As I was curled up in a ball on the medical table, I felt my spine being poked by the needle, and my body reacted spastically. As a result, I noticed I did not have feeling in parts of my right foot. Instead of this problem being an occasional issue on my left, it was now a continuous problem on my right.

Let me describe the sensation in my feet that might make more sense. If you get down on the floor and sit on your feet, sit on them for a long time until it is hard to stand and your feet are numb, not cooperating.

This feeling that likely drives you crazy when you tell others to give you a minute because your feet are asleep. This feeling is much like my numbness every day, all the time. Let's be real. It's a slow, sad reality. I don't seem to fit in, not in the way I formerly belonged. I was evaluating what I could do, and I knew others were wondering the same. My options for treatment were encouraged, but actually seem much scarier than what I was experiencing. A plethora of advice exists: *Here is what you should do. It may or may not help. And when you do take the meds, additional new issues are possible; everyone is different.*

My mind takes me back to that small, sterile medical office, remembering the moment I heard my diagnosis. When I heard about the increased risk of cancer from taking the treatment, my thoughts went to my mom. I mentally shut down after hearing the "c" word. No, thank you, my mom passed away from cancer within three weeks of her diagnosis in 2002 at the age of fifty-seven. I would rather be alive and with my family and deal with the physical struggle than be dead.

The MS diagnosis announcement was similar to my stomach drop while riding the "Demon Drop" at Cedar Point's Amusement Park in Ohio, but this kind of stomach drop was not any fun. The fear of death, though much less prominent among the others, was there as well. I could not leave my family. I needed to be here. My grief for my mother was still very much with me, as was the emptiness that could only be filled by her unconditional love, the special bond, the love of a mother. I couldn't bear the thought of my children going through that.

The MS diagnosis rolled in with a thick fog. I tried to stay ahead of, but it chased me. Before I knew it, I was fully engulfed in the storm. At first, symptoms rumbled like the thunder warning of lightning, the dangerous wind gusts, and the tsunami that may one day overtake me. It began with a light rain that left me soaked, followed by the terrible storm that knocked down my powerlines. *How did I get here? How do I escape? I want to seek shelter, to take control of the ship and steer myself to calm waters, but how? Can my powerlines, my nerves, ever be repaired?* The MS has damaged the myelin sheath, or protective covering around my nerves, so noise and temperature extremes cause them to spark like live wires, constantly jolting me.

### ♩ "Can You Stand the Rain" (New Edition) ♩

Scott and I had been through so much over the past decade. Thank goodness for our kids. They help us weather the storm. The turbulence with the death of both of my parents, my gloomy diagnosis, forecasting an uncertain future of tropical storms or hurricane-force winds. We wonder, *What will the magnitude of my MS actually be? It's just too much to absorb.* I must have had a perpetual blank stare of disbelief on my face. *What does this mean for me and for our family?*

Following my appointment at the Mellon Center, I recall arriving home, turning to my husband to hold and comfort me, sitting curled up in a ball on his lap. We cried together as he held me and wiped my tears. He told me it would be okay, and we would figure it out together. I was consoled by my soulmate, who was "there for me."

### ♩ "I Feel for You" (Chaka Khan) ♩

The fears in my mind were challenging to quiet. I felt emotionally run over. Like I had been dragged into a more confusing time than the accident in 1990. When I was eighteen years old, my femur bone was snapped. It was a clear-cut situation. My broken bone had to be repaired. My body needed time to heal, period. Being physically run over was an inconvenience that shifted my world as I knew it. The physical healing was temporary. I did not fully understand the mental impact, the years of anxiety that the accident would have on my life. Nor did I realize the mental toll that would persevere years after my diagnosis.

I felt anxious. On that day of diagnosis, I began retreating to the hull of a ship. Feeling chained to my diagnosis, I was stuck, being held down, as I felt after the accident in 1990. In 2010 I was in denial, pretending that I was fine. It felt pointless to talk about it. I was not ready to be held down again. *Maybe I can just put this ship, my diagnosis, in neutral.*

Once upon a time, before the accident, my dreams were of visualizing myself walking and strutting the runway as a model. Those dreams felt distant and unattainable after the accident. *I just want to be able to walk again, period, and I did.*

This time is different. I was about to slow down, whether I liked it or not. Multiple sclerosis not only takes a toll on your body, it is a SLOW mind game. What works for some is not guaranteed to work for others. These thoughts were on repeat in my mind and became agonizing. I retreated further into my shell. In *The Call to Courage*, shame researcher, Brené Brown, refers to "the story I'm telling myself." I too was creating a story in my mind; I was uncertain of my abilities, and my confidence had been shaken.

## ♫ "Same Song" (Digital Underground) ♫

Outside of work, I did not have the energy to reach out, to nurture connections, which would have ongoing consequences on some relationships. I was not prepared to face my diagnosis, nor anyone's thoughts on what I should do. I was not prepared to deal with my fatigue either. Thank goodness for the prepared food section at Heinen's grocery store. Our family adapted and found a way to manage. My poor kids had not learned much about cooking from me. They had to buy hot lunch at school. There was no energy at the end of the day to pack lunches or have home-cooked meals. *Maybe one day my family and I should sign up for a cooking class. Or better yet, get an in-home chef… goals.*

My social life, always so important to me, suffered greatly during this decade. I had to face the facts and prioritize my life. I was just not like everyone else, even though I may have appeared very much the same. It was not anyone's fault, but something just had to give. During these years, I felt bad that I did not have the energy to volunteer. No PTO meetings at my kids' school, no energy for extra outings with my kids and their friends. I was never sure how I would feel and how long I could be active before I needed to rest. I was in a pattern of treading water, needing a buoy. I existed, just going through the motions feeling bad and trying to smile, keeping my woes mostly to myself. I wanted to keep up and do what all the cool moms did. Many helped me, even though they were not aware of my diagnosis yet. I just was not ready to face it. I am grateful for so many caring people in my life. These were my "fake it until you make it" years. Chris Bouffard, fellow Educator for the Riverside School District (Painesville, Ohio) and MS Warrior, explains it perfectly, "With MS, you have to fake being well."

I declined invitations from friends and other couples; therefore, those invitations became fewer and farther apart. It is not that I didn't want to socialize, but I could not do it all. I was just struggling to manage my life. I needed to conserve my energy for work and my immediate family time. I missed out too often on volunteering at school as well as connecting with friends and family socially as often as I would have liked. I was just attempting to manage the basics. During this time, I was still processing my situation. I felt exhausted. I would sleep, at times restless. I was less confident in my abilities and, as a result, my social life suffered. I remember, during the school year, folding towels on Saturday afternoons while singing the following song in my head and trying to stay positive.

## ♫ "I'm Every Woman, It's All in Me." (Chaka Khan) ♫

Scott and I would put a plan into action that allowed me to remain focused on family but provided me moments to sneak away and rest.

We would destress during the summer at our weekend retreat in a Private Lake Community in Ashtabula, Ohio, called Roaming Shores. We had the absolute best neighbors at the lake. We looked forward to seeing our "Weekend Family" during the summer months while experiencing mostly unplugged weekends.

Our weekends were for family time while boating, tubing, paddle boats, kayaks, jet skiing, fishing, and napping. We hosted friends and families for a few years, then less often when it became too much. After that, the lake transitioned into more of a family retreat, our escape, if you will. Life needed to slow down. Sitting around the campfire, talking and roasting our marshmallows, and watching our kids catching fireflies under the stars. We would see lots of stars in this dark sky, free of light pollution. We had dinner with our "weekend family" and regularly enjoyed competitive games of "Song Pop."

At the end of an evening, we would settle in the basement to put puzzles together and play cards (like Rummy, Uno, and Garbage), then have movie time and watch John Candy in *The Great Outdoors* on DVD. This was our classic, go-to movie on repeat at the lake. If you ever had a sleepover at the lake house, then you likely remember. We popped popcorn, plugged in the box fan since we had no air conditioning, and snuggled together in "Jimmy Fallon's Ultimate Sac." My mindset would have to strengthen to battle this diagnosis. The lessons that my family and I were about to learn were countless. It was time to make a decision to take the helm and steer the ship.

# PART II

# *Breathe*

# Chapter Five
## Be Present

**Take a Chill Pill**

Focusing on the present, it was unrealistic for me to plan my MS and map out my route for the course of my life. There may be storms ahead, but right now the sun was shining, and my symptoms were at bay, fairly manageable. Time to live for the moment and focus on my *I cans*. Prior to my diagnosis, Scott and I had made the agreement to take action in life. Our plan was to travel for a significant anniversary trip every five years as a couple.

- Honeymoon: 1994 The Bahamas

- 5-Year: 1999 cruise the Hawaiian Islands

- 10-Year: 2004 St. Thomas, St. John

- 15-Year: 2009 Riviera Maya, Mexico

This was the last trip just a month before the Pirate Triathlon that would lead to my diagnosis. I treasure these pictures, which include some "badass" shots of me." I look at that thirty-eight-year-old girl, so calm, confident and self-assured, unaware of the turbulent waters ahead.

By December 2013, we brought home our first standard poodle puppy, Cosmo, who melted the hearts of our family. He was a sweet boy and really behaved like a therapy dog. Cosmo was born October 13, 2013, our go-with-the-flow "velcro" dog, loved and adored by all. Since we are fans of Larry David's sitcom, *Seinfeld,* Cosmo was named after the character, Kramer. Cosmo is his first name.

In August 2015, Clarence "Clancy" William Lohrey, Scott's Dad, Papa, lost his battle with colon cancer. Here are two vivid memories to give you a snapshot of my father-in-law. When I was twenty, I had traveled to Mentor, Ohio, to see Scott, who was home on a college break. After a solo four-hour drive, I rang the doorbell and waited on the front porch of the colonial-style home with red brick on the bottom and white aluminum siding on top. The windows were nestled between black shutters, with a single tall candle lit in each window. Clancy opened the front door of their home.

He appeared to be eating an apple out of his massive hand, but as he continued to take bites of it, I realized it was not an apple but, instead, a head of raw cabbage! *Have you ever seen anyone choose to eat a head of raw cabbage like that?!* He was eating one leaf of cabbage at a time and then alternating bites right into the cabbage. I have no recollection of the actual conversation. I was distracted, watching him peel away the layers. His dad was massive and muscular, just a large human. I was told when Scott was in elementary school, some kids thought his dad was "Popeye."

The other memory was when Clancy was home with hospice care, nearly on his deathbed. "Papa," as he was called by his grandkids, would sit on his 2004 John Deere 4400 tractor one last time. This tractor had a large bucket on the front and a mowing attachment on the back. Papa was on his tractor with the help of my fifteen-year-old son, Alex. Alex took charge of operating the tractor, reaching up to the levers while standing on the ground. Papa could just sit in the seat observing. Papa, usually the operating expert, must have felt human to be outside, involved in "work" he did his whole life. He was surely proud to be watching his grandson in action.

Thankfully, he taught his grandson everything he needed to know about this piece of equipment. Alex moved thousands of pounds of steel from the backyard onto a trailer while Papa supervised. Within days Papa's body would further fail; this once-strong man was deteriorating. He was not talking, just lying in his hospice bed. Immediate family, relatives, and close friends had all said goodbye to Dad, Papa, Clancy respectively. He was no longer talking, but his body was restless. Day after day, he still was hanging on, his body in conflict. During his final days, our former neighbor and friend came to visit. Pastor Potter prayed for Papa along with us. Though appearing to be sleeping, Papa would randomly utter, "I gotta go!"

Next, Alex suggested so clearly: *Why don't we all tell him that we will meet him there?* And so we did. Later that same night, August 17, 2015, Papa relaxed and passed peacefully. Clarence William Lohrey has truly left a void in the Lohrey family.

That same year, I found myself in the multi-functional waiting room of the Independent Stem Cell Research Center and Office of Plastic Surgery. I was so happy to sit in this waiting room. It was a beautifully lit, bright, and welcoming waiting room. Other people in the waiting room did not know that I had MS. For all anyone knew, I was there for fillers or a boob job. Now, this is a positive headspace for me, and no, I don't have a boob job or fillers, in case you wondered… "Not that there's anything wrong with that!" (*Seinfeld:* The Outing Episode, 1993)

Being a participant in the stem cell research study was the correct choice for me. It was successful in that the lesions on my brain did not change. In addition, I just felt better, with more energy. My best way to describe it was like I drank the youth potion in the movie, *Death Becomes Her,* starring Bruce Willis, Meryl Streep, and Goldie Hawn. I only wished that feeling lasted longer.

## ♪ "Breathe" (Faith Hill) ♪

# Chapter Six
# *Facts*

*I* highly suggest that you read *Let Me Hold You Longer* by Karen Kingsbury. This children's book captures the essence of life with your kids, as if you knew your experiences as they were growing up were the last. Warning: For me, reading this children's book has always been a tear jerker.

Scott and I chose to live each family trip like it was our last. We explored and took adventures and said yes to everything possible. If there was an obstacle, then we would make attempts to discover another way. We were never sure what I would be able to do from year to year. Our belief, like the Nike slogan "JUST DO IT," impacted us greatly.

Our checklist became more urgent. Our family belief was to live life to the fullest, do what we can with what we have while we are able. Scott was forty-five, I was forty-four, Alex was fifteen, and Aryn was thirteen. There was no time to waste. Time to live in the present. Life is too short to wait for the perfect time. I recall my father's advice, "Don't waste time." MS was a gift that brought a new sense of focus. MS taught us not to take time for granted. Instead of having an "I have to" mindset, my thoughts shift into an "I get to" mindset.

## ♪ "Good Day" (Nappy Roots) ♪

## "Just Do It" Trip #1: Grand Canyon (Las Vegas)

As a kid, I remember sitting on the floor in my mom's room, sliding back the door of her side of the closet and looking at her shoes. They rested, carefully placed on a two-tier gold metal plated shoe rounder. Now I was understanding fully why Mom's shoe rack looked as it did, filled with shoes that would attach to her feet. In 2015, my shoes started to evolve into straps around the ankles or tennis shoes. Shoes needed to be secured to my feet. I was a fashionista at heart, so it pained me to let go of so many cute shoes that were no longer practical. *Will I ever wear cute shoes again?*

Next on the bucket list was a helicopter ride. Scott said we could take a much quicker trip by air. Grand Canyon SkyWalk, here we come. The horseshoe-shaped cantilever bridge with the glass walkway was on the Indian Reservation on the west rim of the Grand Canyon. The skywalk was an absolutely breathtaking experience. We were so high above the Colorado River. Two seemingly small patches of grass four thousand feet below, we learned, were actually two football fields in length. I looked at my face in the pictures. I appear so happy and walking independently. Next, we would visit the Red Rock Canyon National Conservation Area. It was a great connection to nature, the kids climbed, and I took pictures. I was able to walk the path, skip the climb, lean or sit on the boulders, take the pictures, then rest again in the car.

## "Just Do It" Trip #2: Grand Cayman Island (June 2016)

The Westin on Seven Mile Beach was the most picturesque, pristine beach with powdery white sand that I had ever seen in my life. It got even better once I stepped into these warm waters; they were so clear I could see my feet on the sandy bottom. The peaceful rhythmic sounds of the waves crashing and then rolling onto the shore were so serene. I felt alive. I could breathe and enjoy these spectacular sights.

# 6 | FACTS

> *Pause. Take a deep breath and travel to the ocean shore, your feet in the warm water, the grit of sand between your toes, the sound of the waves rolling onto shore, the sun on your face, and the warm breeze. Do you feel it? Breathe in. Breathe out.*

This trip held new adventures for the kids; it was their first snorkeling experience. From the shoreline near our hotel, we walked out into the ocean and submerged our bodies, and began to explore the world underwater. Flippers on, masks in place, snorkels in the air, we began to float; Aryn screamed into the mask, *"Ah Fiisshhhh!!!"* I heard her underwater. I'm choking, laughing, and treading water. I responded, *"Honey, we are trying to see the fish."* Let's just say she was not expecting the numerous, colorful fish right at our fingertips.

Another day, on the catamaran excursion to Stingray City, we met lots of Stingrays, including Frisbee, who was missing his tail. Stingray City was the crystal-clear, warm waters in the sandbar in the middle of the ocean where you can meet the stingrays. *Kiss a stingray on the nose for seven years of good luck. Check.*

My husband was very aware of my sticking points when booking excursions. Scott assured me there would be a bathroom on the catamaran. This was something that was an issue for me with my MS. The struggle was real, and the availability of a bathroom was a constant question.

The next item to check off the list was to take a walk on the beach with my daughter. Our resort was on Seven Mile Beach. Let's be real, my intention was not to walk Seven Miles, but I did desire to take a stroll with my daughter. The morning sun reflected off the turquoise water with a warm, gentle breeze as Aryn and I began our walk through the powdery white sand on the beach. As we made it past a few resorts, the walking caused fatigue affecting my left leg. As my leg began to drag, I knew I had to rest on the beach. Aryn sat down on the beach with me. "I may have pushed myself a little too much," I admitted to her. *How can I make it back?* Mom always said, *"Where there is a will, there is a way."*

I was not calling Scott to admit he was right and that it was too much for me.

Aryn continued her return walk on the beach as I enjoyed my solution to my problem. Fully clothed, I got into the ocean while floating and swimming back to our hotel. Once I was near our resort, Aryn had to help me exit the ocean. I may have dripped a trail of water in the hotel on our way back to the room, but I made it back. *When walking is challenging, I can swim.*

I was smiling ear to ear and giggling to myself, so happy to make my way back. *I will never give up; there is always a way.*

## "Just Do It" Trip #3: Las Vegas, Nevada (July 2016)

The kayaking excursion with our family down the Colorado River from Willow Beach in Arizona was on our list. We were equipped with water guns and paddles to cool off from the one-hundred-eighteen-degree temperatures. *Destination: Emerald Cave*, a gorgeous cave accessible only by water. Once we backed our kayaks into the cave, the reflections revealed the stunning emerald cave and waters. It was so magnificent; the location has been photographed in *National Geographic Magazine*.

## Rekt

Live life, do it now while you are able. The next opportunity: our tour guide invited our group to either rest on the small beach area or experience cliff jumping. The climb to the top of a boulder seemed several stories high. As I looked up to the top, then next to me, my teenage kids were right with me, a bit nervous about me climbing. I promised to take my time using both my hands and my feet. I was nervous about my ability too, but *I can! I must!* I was saying yes to these opportunities. I had to try. *This may be my last. Be brave.*

The tour guide was with us while the rest of the tour group decided to pass on this adventure. The guide instructed us to jump out to avoid the rocks below. Scott had stayed below to film as each of the kids took turns leaping out and making it look so easy.

At the top, the pull of gravity was intense; my legs were quite shaky, and unsteady. "Jump out," our guide said. There was no "jumping" required. As I left the stone behind, I felt the swift pull to the earth so forceful. Within seconds I splashed into the brisk fifty-seven-degree water. I did it! Cliff jump, *check. How do the cliff divers do it? The force of gravity against your body is incredible. #respect for cliff jumpers.*

Our kids were quickly and continuously climbing and jumping. Scott and I switched spots. He carefully and thoughtfully ascended the huge boulder for his jump. He stood at the very top, peered out, and realized that it was much higher than it appeared. As I witnessed his hesitation, I called out some encouragement. "*C'mon honey, you can do it!*"

He scratched his head, looked back, evaluating the climb back down, then leaned to look over the cliff's edge at the water below. The guide warned, "Whatever you do, don't dive!" Then gravity took over and pulled him over the cliff. Too late, he fell. The first body part to enter the water was his right arm, followed by his left hand, his head, his body, and lastly, Scott's feet. *How is this possible?* Exactly what Scott was trying to avoid.

"Ouch!"

"Are you okay, honey?" I said.

Scott laughed it off and said he was fine, but he had hit the water with such force that his cheek, the one on his face, was bleeding. We caught the fall on video, and oh how we laughed until we cried. We laughed because he was okay, of course. When faced with a decision, hesitation may not serve you. It's best to take advice from those that have done it before. Don't overthink it. Jump in!

## ♪ "Jump" (Van Halen) ♪

Later that year, Scott had the idea that we should get another dog; he thought Cosmo, our first standard poodle, was lonely. Scott called our breeder and learned they were planning to mate Cosmo's parents one last time; therefore, I reluctantly agreed, and he put us on the list.

On September 13, 2016, Leo and his littermates were born. Our second Red Standard Poodle. Leo's mom was the same, but Leo had a different dad from Cosmo. The story: Cosmo's parents mated, but apparently, their new stud decided to take a turn with Mom while she was still in heat. When the pups were born, DNA testing revealed that *most* of them were from Cosmo's dad! *Two different dads for the same litter? I did not know this was possible.*

With our position on the list, we ended up with the other dad's pup. Cosmo was just like his father, sitting like royalty and a protector. Leo was also like his father, a licker. Leo was such a good-looking pup but slept through anything, unaware of what was happening. Our "Uncle" Leo was named after Jerry's uncle from *Seinfeld*. Leo would salivate and vomit during car rides as a puppy, yet Cosmo was always a great car rider. Cosmo chilled, waited patiently for us, and just nudged his head into your hand to greet you. Leo, on the other hand, leaped like a pogo stick to say, "Hell- loooo" like Uncle Leo from *Seinfeld*; he was right in your face, saying, "Look at me," demanding attention. Cosmo licked when there was something to lick. Leo licked all the time, including his infamous "air licking." It was obvious that your nature made a difference, whether dog or human. My fur babies can each be described with their own special song. We love them both dearly.

**Cosmo:**
**♫ "Me and My Shadow" ♫**
**(Frank Sinatra & Sammy Davis Jr.)**

**"Uncle" Leo:**
**♫ "JUMP" ♫**
**(Kris Kross)**

## "Just Do It" Trip #4: Key West, Duck Key, and Fort Lauderdale (2017)

We swam with the dolphins in Duck Key, but walking to really explore Key West was not a viable option for me, which was frustrating. *In the past, I used to be the "fast walker," the one being asked to slow down, but now it is challenging for me to keep up. I have to learn more patience with myself.* It was exhausting, like I was carrying around a weighted blanket with a concentrated effect on the left side of my body. In Key West, Scott rented an electric golf cart, so "I can" too. The whole family would ride instead, which ended up being fun. Before my mother passed in 2002, she gave us a gift of remembrance. She said when you see a butterfly think of me. Next stop, the Butterfly Conservatory for a beautiful, peaceful afternoon with the butterflies.

Fort Lauderdale would be the final destination for this trip, a full day and night of family time with my brother Jon, his wife Janet, and nephew George. Beach time, pool time, a life-size chess game, and take-out was the perfect way to fill my cup. A nice time with family at my pace. *I can too, in an alternate way. Our family time just chillin' is just my speed.*

## "Just Do It" Trip #5: Kauai, Hawaii (2018)

Awakened by the local roosters, we began our trip with an early-morning bike ride; we pedaled a regular bike with two wheels up the coastal bike path. Next, a trip to the local farmer's market. Our family chatted with a gentleman who was selling freshly picked coconut, papaya, mango, and pineapple. He said he was seventy-seven years young and still climbing trees for the coconuts. His advice: *"Be happy; have fun!"*

What began with the thought of capturing a couple of pictures turned into a two-mile hike in Waimea Canyon. My idea was sparked by the sign in the parking lot pointing to the waterfall. Laser-focused, some might say stubborn, I wanted to go. Realistic or not, I must try. My eyes widened, dreaming of this waterfall. I knew it would be a challenge, but I was determined. You can't tell me no. "Let's do it!" I say, smiling, "C'mon, please. It won't take us too long." I tried to convince my husband, who reluctantly followed. I actually underestimated the time and the hiking ability needed to get to the falls, although I was not about to admit it during the hike. Through the trees, over the rocks; they were really boulders. During the hike, Scott was frustrated with me, to put it nicely. We were not at all prepared for this hike.

Our parent-child roles had to be reversed for my survival. We needed our kids to lead the way. It was obvious that I was slowing down and needed assistance. Alex searched and found me the perfect hiking stick from the woods and took my hand as he navigated the safest path for me to climb over the boulders.

## ♫ "Trouble" (Lindsey Buckingham) ♫

If you have been to Kauai, then you would be familiar with the "Original Red Dirt" shirts that can be purchased on the island. I wore the Kauai Red Dirt on more than just my shirt. We made it to the waterfall to capture family pictures and memories. On the hike back, Scott was less than enthused that we were miles from the car without water. Alex navigated the path and the boulders in a way that reminded me of Mario from the Super Mario Bros video game. He would easily leap from boulder to boulder.

About halfway back, Alex volunteered to run ahead to the car to get our bottles of water. Scott and I told Aryn she could go with him since we are so slow. Our kids took charge. Aryn vigorously refused to go with Alex. "Mom, if I leave you, you will fall off the cliff." Aryn stayed right by my side, like the parent, and kept me on the inside, away from the cliff's edge, while Alex increased the pace of his hike to at least triple our pace.

Mahalo (thank you) to my Ohana (family); they assisted me in accomplishing this hike.

Although I knew the hike was not realistic, in my heart, I was concerned, I had to do it now or lose the opportunity for life. I felt the "feels" of strong love and protection for me as a mother and wife. The protectiveness revealed in frustration from my hubby, as evidenced in a picture I captured where his hand is smacked against his forehead, like, "Oh no, here she goes again"; it makes me giggle. I was thrilled with RED, dirt all over my body from sliding down a couple of hills like a turtle on her back. I was a disheveled and delighted "mess," smiling ear to ear. *I did it! I can, with help from my family.*

## ♫ "Lean On Me" (Bill Withers) ♫

### Get Naked

The next day the surf was strong for our beach day at Poipu Beach, boogie boarding with the turtles. We grabbed a delicious lunch at Breneke's Deli and Restaurant, a favorite near the beach. Then Scott,

Alex, and Aryn enjoyed the waves with the huge turtles that were surfing right next to them. The turtles startled them at first glance, but they realized the turtles just wanted to play too.

"Mom, you're not getting in the water (ocean) here! No offense, but you will die." I actually had enough adventure the day before during the hike, so I rested on the beach. *I agree. No offense taken.* While I watched safely from my rented beach chair, Scott and the kids had an amazing time. They would each take breaks to hang with me and recap their adventure. "Mom, did you see that?" They loved the turtles, like hang ten, dude, but in real life.

A fit young lady in her twenties body-surfing appeared to be having a great time, then she rolled up on the shore, stunned and naked! Her entire bathing suit had been completely stripped off and swept away by the waves. This was not a nude beach. My decision to pass on the swim was confirmed.

On Father's Day, we embarked on a journey to set sail on a catamaran for snorkeling off the Napali Coast. We traveled up the coastline where they filmed the Jurassic Park movies. The crew anchored the catamaran, then we all jumped in. Aryn and I explored, hand-in-hand, equipped with our snorkeling gear. Faces in the water, our snorkels in the air, flippers flipping as we held hands, and then the ocean floor just dropped off. The current pushed us toward the dark, where the ocean floor was no longer visible. My stomach dropped as I gazed out and attempted to resist the push of the current. *Reverse, reverse! This massive endless ocean, an eerie unknown depth, felt much like my diagnosis. I only wish I could put my MS progression in reverse.*

We made it safely and swam back to the catamaran and enjoyed the ride back. Our lovely day was topped off with hand-dipped ice cream from "Tropical Dreams" and a beautiful sunset.

## ♫ "The Sound of Sunshine" (Michael Franti) ♫

# Chapter Seven
## The Call

**Fall 2018**

My quote as an educator was inspired on opening day before returning to work for the new school year. A call to action by our assistant superintendent that left an imprint on my heart was to search for a meaningful quote to live by, but it was a struggle for me. We were told we should "live our banner" and make a difference in our twenty square feet. *What "banner" do I live by?* For days and into the next week, this thought was on replay in my mind. I seek help from my friend and fellow school counselor.

**It Always Works Out**

"Kathy, I'm really struggling with choosing my quote." Mrs. Francis, our scheduling guru, was feverishly working on the master schedule in order to have all of the issues corrected before the first day of school. She was an excellent counselor, but today there was no time for counseling. The start of the school year was quickly approaching, and the last item she needed was to help me find a quote. She was the one in checklist mode attending to our deadline while I was in my head. As Kathy and I would always say, "It always works out." *It really worked out. Things happen for a reason, and her advice "works out."* While simultaneously attending to her computer screen, without even turning around, she continued working and directed me. "See the book of quotes on the shelf?" *Yes.* She continued, "Just take that book, open it, and the quote that you open up to is your quote." Here were the words I would live by:

## "In a gentle way, you can shake the world."
## – Mahatma Gandhi

*I'm just a middle school counselor. Bewildered. How can I possibly shake the world? How would I live my quote?* During our opening assembly at LaMuth Middle School, I put out a call to action with hundreds of my middle school students, asking them to think about how they might "shake the world" in the future. Yet I was still searching to identify how my quote was meant to impact my life. I was puzzled; I was not in a headspace to believe in myself and my own abilities. I began to feel ashamed and embarrassed that I was not keeping up, feeling that what I had to say was not important. I was distracted, without a vision bigger than my private health issues, my school, and my community. I admitted to my students that I was unsure of how **I** could "shake the world." Possibly there was some way that I could inspire them to live their purpose, and as a result, they would impact the world.

During my smaller classroom career lessons, I would enter the room rolling my carry-on luggage behind me, asking students to make sure their seats and tray tables were in the proper position for take-off. I asked them to use the clues. "What do you think I wanted to be when I was your age?" The answer was a flight attendant.

Then I would ask students and teachers alike to close their eyes. "Imagine your life fifteen years from now." I asked students to "picture" or "visualize" how they imagined their future, beginning with waking up to their alarms in the morning, picturing their surroundings and how they would be getting dressed for the day (i.e., uniform, casual, a dress, a suit?). I asked these twelve-year-olds to "think of working a job for three times your lifetime." It was important for me to spark ideas to help them begin to uncover what they liked to do, what they were good at, and what career would support the lifestyle they wanted. My goals were to inspire students to start the search for a career that would make them feel fulfilled in life. Then we worked backward, starting with their dream, then figuring out how they could make it a reality and live the lives they wanted to live. They would write down the path they chose and their goals for the future.

Focused on her own future, my daughter Aryn wrote a reflection of my triathlon race day in 2009, drafting ideas for college essays in her English class, sharing the lessons she had learned. Here is how my daughter remembers the experience of my triathlon sprint day and beyond, from when she was only seven.

## "A Meaningful Life" (written by Aryn Lohrey)

In 2009, I stood with my dad and my brother in Fairport Harbor, Ohio, at the Pirate Triathlon, supporting my mother. It was a breezy, sunny day. The wind was blowing off the lake right past our faces. We were wearing black, long-sleeved shirts to support her. At that time, I did not know that my life would be changed forever. After observing her difficulty running across the finish line, I knew something wasn't right. She spent the next twelve months, with the help of doctors, trying to uncover what was hidden inside of her, what was causing the imbalance of her body.

The following summer, 2010, my mom was diagnosed with multiple sclerosis. Watching my mother be impacted by this degenerative disease has changed my life and the way I look at life. I have learned to Never Give Up, to have gratitude for the simple things in life, and acceptance that everyone has some challenges to overcome.

The inspiration to keep going, the biggest incentive to get things done, and the courage to never give up are the lessons I have learned through my upbringing. These lessons were not told to me through a conversation; instead, I learned them through watching my mother. Every morning I wake up, hearing the sound of feet smacking on the ground and walking down the steps to find my mom on the treadmill at 5:30 a.m. pushing herself to finish her workout. *"I won't be able to do this one day,"* she says, as I watch her in admiration, and I think of how proud I am of her, considering most that are able wouldn't dare to work as hard as she does.

Most people, like myself, take for granted the simple things that I could not imagine not doing again. My biggest role model, the one who is always there for me, gets torn at the idea of walking. Countless times walking through the mall and having to take breaks, to times when she is tripping everywhere. It gets hard to sit back and watch. At times I was in denial that she needed help getting back to the car, hoping and praying this would go away.

As I started growing up, I realized that my mom does need help and it's okay. Not only do I have a closer relationship with her, I now have a greater understanding of what she is going through. How she feels when she says she is tired. The explanation that she feels like there are weights tied to her feet has a huge impact on the way I think. The slightest bit of help gives her more confidence in the way she does things and keeps her going for longer.

Many see walking as an easy task, but complications hold my mom back from doing so. My ability to push past this disease puts me where I am today. I have learned to cherish the times I have and never take time for granted. Nobody will be able to understand the feelings she gets except her. I strive to make the most of every second. My mom's feelings push me to not care about the opinions of others but to be who I truly am. She makes me strive to find the importance in all parts of my life, from small ones to big ones.

## Low-Key

For years I had felt bad that I had M.S. and couldn't keep up, unable to do the things that other parents were physically able to do. I had no energy for the extras. I missed out on the fun stuff like traveling to visit family and friends and other activities, including events to support nieces and nephews. I really wanted to do everything, but I was unsure of myself, my ability. I was exhausted, so it was challenging to look past the couch. Embarrassed by my lack of energy, I always believed it was important to be a hard worker so I never wanted to be perceived as lazy. Maybe I could just disappear under the blanket for a bit.

But as I reflect, M.S. has really been a gift that taught my children some of the most important lessons of all. Never Give Up! Work Together. Help Each Other. Be Brave. Face it. Allow frustration to fuel the determination to overcome the challenge. Feel the feels, release the emotion, tearfully at times, then try and find your own way. Discover new ways to feel accomplished and achieve success. I knew how to be empathetic with others, but I needed to practice patience and be kinder to myself. Face my limitations, be real about them. I needed to learn to accept myself.

### ♫ "Joy and Pain" (Rob Base) ♫

## "Just Do It" Trip #6: Maui, Hawaii (2019)

For our twenty-fifth wedding anniversary, Scott and I renewed our vows on the beach. I was not expecting my tears as Alex and Aryn witnessed our union the second time around.

### ♫ "Stuck On You" (Lionel Richie) ♫

We knew this might be the last time just the four of us traveled together since Aryn would be graduating from high school in 2020. At this time, we had no clue that the pandemic would be altering life as we knew it.

In 2020, Hawaii would not have even been an option; travel bans were in effect.

On the road to Hana, Aryn offered me her arm to get to the "Seven Pools." Locking arms with my daughter, her kindness made me smile and provided me with extra support and confidence; she kept me on the right path.

> *FYI: If you ever are walking with Aryn and me, you may notice her keen ear for my left foot beginning to flop. Her head may snap back if she is walking in front of me. She knows immediately when I am tired; there is no denying it with her. She is protective like a mama bear.*

Our mother-daughter bond is an empowering one. We support each other and have real heart-to-heart conversations. She had been curious and wanted to know how I felt. "Mom, do you feel sad that you can't run anymore?" My answer: "I am happy to get to watch you run." *Let's be real, I would like to do more than I do, but I'm okay being the bystander when it comes to running. It's time for me to participate differently in life.*

## Hey, Coach

In the summer of 2019, Aryn played travel lacrosse with the Burning River girls' travel lacrosse team with Coach Todd. We had returned from our trip from Hawaii and were set to travel with Aryn's team to Indianapolis, Indiana. (Aryn had picked up a lacrosse stick for the first time the night before tryouts her freshman year of high school, yet she had a love for the sport and a natural instinct to play.) Some things in life just seem "meant to be." On our way to Indiana, we arranged to attend Youngstown State University's "Preview Days" on June 28,

2019. Aryn was wearing her U.S. lacrosse shirt, and President Jim Tressel noticed. He said he had just hired a women's lacrosse coach days before. President Tressel then asked where we were from; the answer was Mentor, Ohio. He was also from Mentor. After a little more conversation, Scott tells President Tressel that his father, Clancy, used to play football for his dad, Lee Tressel, at Baldwin Wallace. As it turns out, Scott's dad knew "Jimmy" Tressel in his youth, and President, aka Coach Tressel, remembered Scott's dad too! It was a comforting connection to pursue this University for school and lacrosse.

## Deadass

It was the end of August, and the weather was still nice so I wore sandals to work that strapped to my feet. When I bent down at the start of the day to put my lunch in the office refrigerator, *My pinky toe is outside of my sandal. Wait, what?* I showed my friend Keley that my toe was out of my sandal; we had a good laugh about that. At the time, it was quite funny, but the disturbing reality was that I did not even feel my toe. No clue this was happening, I had put my sandals on at home, drove to school, walked into the building, and finally noticed my toe by seeing it on the outside of my sandal. *Seriously, what the hell? What are you doing out there?*

I was one of two middle school counselors, and when the students came back to school, I was exhausted. I frequently put a smile on my face and pushed through, but by noon I recognized my stamina was low. I was forgetting tasks, and work, in general, became more and more stressful; I was aware of my inefficiencies. My checklist became overwhelming, and my symptoms more noticeable.

Each task that caused any level of stress was accompanied by my friends," the optical floaters." The floaters used to just come to visit on occasion, and now they were "dropping in" my field of vision quite frequently. As a result, my sight was impaired to the point that on one particular day, I walked straight into the corner of my office door. So let me explain this. My door was halfway open, about forty-five degrees. The floaters and spots had disrupted my vision so much that I didn't even see the door. I recall trying to leave my office, unaware the door was half-open. This was a wake-up call. Thankfully I managed to stay on my feet, but I was shaken and startled at the decline.

By the end of the week, friends and coworkers were discussing plans for the weekend, getting together, or traveling. What had changed over the years? I didn't even make plans or attempt to engage in these conversations. *Why?* It made me sad because I did not have the energy to do anything extra. I no longer had the endurance to work during the week and was not even considering socializing for a gathering locally, let alone traveling on a weekend.

At work, I was losing confidence in myself and my abilities. I was no longer using the stairs as I had become a fall risk. We disguised my need for walking assistance with a rolling table that was hiding my "green hair." We just found a way for me to function. Work just became overwhelming to the point where it was time for the task of researching, consulting, and filing for disability. This made me so sad.

I was torn, aware that I was not functioning in my usual way. There was a disconnect. I began feeling burdensome, a liability, yet was not ready to leave my career. I did not want to "give up," even though my feet were numb, often swelling, I would attempt to elevate them under my desk on top of my garbage can. My hands began to shake more, making it challenging to steady them enough to dial the phone to return calls. At times, when I got progressively tired, my speech was impaired. It became more difficult to understand me. I was aware, so I would slow my speech, which became annoying to myself and others. I was not processing my thoughts as quickly, so I was slower at communicating my ideas. If you have ever worked in a school, you know there just wasn't time for me to take my time. My input began to feel irrelevant. I just wasn't processing fast enough and getting my words

## 7 | THE CALL

out in a timely manner. I literally slept my evenings away. I was giving every ounce of effort at work and feeling like it was subpar. My tank was empty by the time I got home.

Being an educator for twenty-five years, the role of middle school counselor was more than a job to me, more than a career. It was part of me, my identity. By acknowledging my areas of difficulty, and facing that my challenges affected me and everyone around me, I was losing myself. *Why me?* When I completed the disability paperwork, I felt like I had lost once again. I was preparing to mourn my job, my career, my life as I knew it. My socialization, my confidence, was being stripped away a little bit at a time. M.S. was not a death sentence but a slow and ongoing punishment. I felt like the "at-risk" kid in school who was always getting into trouble. Something was always being taken away, no matter how hard I tried.

My calling in life was being a counselor for middle school students. I continued to make myself available as a counselor for the needs of students, families, teachers, administration, and the community as much as possible. I had always enjoyed my career and felt needed, being a problem-solver. I felt valuable; however, it was taking a noticeable toll on me.

It was a struggle to keep my eyes open by the end of the workday, especially during the commute home, even though the drive was only twenty minutes. My own family easily recalls times when I would arrive home, lay on the couch, and literally nod off in the middle of conversations, exhausted. Plenty of times when my husband or my kids were talking to me, I would have so many thoughts to share but lacked the energy to respond in a timely manner or at all.

I recall thinking, *This must be how someone in a coma feels.*

Most times resting and napping would help reboot my system, simply lying still just like a corpse. But it was taking longer for me to recover from my workday. I did not want to face my disease. A combination of uncertainty, embarrassment, and denial led me to mentally not accepting my degeneration.

My personal family life suffered because I lacked the energy or the patience to be the mom, wife, friend, daughter-in-law, sister, sister-in-law, aunt, or niece that I desired to be. I didn't feel like myself. *My family deserves so much more from me, as I deserve more time with them.* I felt impatient, cranky, and sad about my lack of energy and participation in life. I felt like I was losing control of my body and my mind.

## ♫ "Bitch" (Meredith Brooks) ♫

I was grateful to my coworkers who had compassion for my challenges and helped me. Let's just say I was aware that I was not keeping up. My career, as I had known it, was too much. The pain of judgment, the extra glances, was humbling. I cared what people thought. It's hard to deal with the comments and the questions as your issues become more recognizable. I tried to smile and focus on what *I can do*.

Then December 28, 2019, the letter arrived: disabled. This was a tough pill to swallow, especially after all my years of service, rather than retiring with pride and a celebration of my accomplishments like other educators in the past. This letter brought shame and embarrassment that my body could not make it to the proper retirement expectations of thirty-five years. The letter essentially told me, "*I can't.*" It also gave me just three days to clean out my office.

One day I was an integral part of the team, and the next day I was out.

*Pause. Breathe.*

*What was my purpose?* My abilities were not the same as in the past. My "I cans" and Never Give Up approach to life had to find a new path.

I started a list of ideas of things *I can* do. Maybe I would start writing children's books, or drawing and painting. *I really should have taken art classes.* I included scrapbooking on my list, but I had already made each of my kids scrapbooks for just about every year of their lives. In addition, I made digital family vacation books for the "Just Do It" trips. I planned to start reading more. Still making my list, I added learning to cook.

Now I would adjust to a gentle fitness practice with yoga, light weights, and a stationary bike. The treadmill and the elliptical were just too much these days. It pained me because I had been a dedicated cardio girl for years, doing it five to seven times per week. I needed to feel accomplished, I needed to have goals. I was proud (and still am) to have commemorative shirts to prove my accomplishments. My days of pedaling to the point, teaching spinning class, and the triathlon sprint remain enjoyable memories. I remember them fondly.

# Chapter Eight
## *Believe*

**January 2020**
**Shook**

Being an educator was part of my life for a quarter-century, my identity. *Now, what?* I pivoted and said yes to joining my friend, Keley Meredith, for a vision board class led by Lindsey Sadowski in Mentor, Ohio. Lindsey, who is an NET (Neuro Emotional Technique) practitioner, gave us a demo of NET and then the guidelines for creating a vision board. Keley and I were both scrapbookers, so we were looking forward to crafting. I had no job, no direction. Since education was no longer an option, I had a blank canvas to create. I loved the pictures in the magazines, the crafting, approaching it with no preconceived ideas. *What do I want to attract into my life?*

I turned to Keley, telling her, "I really don't understand why the hell I'm pulling some of these pictures since I don't have a job anymore." This was not a thinking project. This was a feeling project. At some point, we felt compelled to send a "selfie" to our friend, school psychologist, and former lunch buddy, Jim Wank. When our break was over, we resumed creating our future.

♫ **"Feels"** ♫
**(Calvin Harris, feat. Pharrell Williams,**
**Katy Perry & Big Sean)**

## Bet

My Vision Board: January 2020:

- Your future looks rosy, find Wellness

- "All our dreams can come true if we have the courage to pursue them." – Walt Disney

- Ignite Brilliance, Choose Your Powerful, Enjoy the Freedom.

- "Every single day, do something that makes your heart sing." –Marcia Wieder

- Dressed to the Nines, Fashionable Color

- Live Life in Color, Own it, Glow Boost

- Inspire; You're awesome, Badass!

- "The Subtle Art of Not Giving a F*ck," by Mark Manson

- Daily health: YOU, ONLY BETTER.

- Power Couples Do Good Together.

- Unforgettable, Find the Beauty in You

- Legendary, Events, Going Places, Choose Your Path

- Stay Strong; Glow Getter; Brighter

- Discover What Lies Beyond the Expected.

- • PLAY. LEARN. DISCOVER.

ENERGIZE &
Refresh
EAT STRONG
FAMILY
LOVE
THIS
YEAR
FEEL
great
peaceful
EXPERIENCE
VIBRATIONS
an
ageless
spirit
retreats
DISCOVER
what lies
BEYOND
the expected
OUTSIDE OF
ORDINARY
fit
Capture

Lindsey's approach to the vision board was "Manifest positive change in your life using a vision board and Neuro-Emotional Technique," which, she said, was a "modern twist to the traditional vision board class." How was it different? Lindsey Sadowski muscle-tested each participant for all pictures on the board to make sure their brain and body were "congruent with your vision." Basically, she really cleared up the subconscious. If someone's subconscious was stuck, she'd use Neuro-Emotional Technique to identify the issue, to be uncovered later in NET sessions if they chose.

Once our boards were created, Lindsey muscle-tested us, then we signed our boards. *Check.*

By March 2020, the pandemic was in full effect in the United States and affecting the schools in our area. My egocentric perception was that the world had shut down to help me adjust. *It's time for me to accept my journey.* A "get real" conversation began to happen about our home. Alex had graduated, and Aryn would soon graduate. Our house had become too big, too much for me, for the two of us. It was time to face reality.

In April, our pre-loved home was put on the market. It was custom-built, designed with spacious bedrooms and walk-in closets. A perfect home for hosting family and friends, with a fantastic area for fun in the sun, complete with an inground pool with a curvy slide, a diving board, and a pool house. It was also conveniently located with park access from the property, within walking distance to the middle school and high school, and so much more. Our lovely home held so many beautiful memories, but it was time for a new family to love and find joy within its walls. Our home sold quickly, and we moved to the lake, Roaming Shores, full-time.

In the following month, July, I was introduced to a "Twosie." My mindset shifted during an appointment with my medical massage therapist. Prior to that, I noticed that my therapist, Heather, had been posting a lot about nails on Facebook. Walking up the sidewalk for my appointment, I thought, *I really hope she doesn't try to talk to me about the nails.* During the massage, there was a pause in our conversation, and I am still in disbelief at what I said.

I was the one who initiated the nail conversation, saying, "So, tell me about this nail stuff you're doing." *Oh, nooooo! Wait, what did I just say?* But it was too late. She was already offering to put a "twosie" tester on my finger. I said, "No, that's okay." I continued making excuses; my nails were so bad.

I thought I had it all figured out. In pictures, I would simply tuck my fingers under, hide them in my pockets or place my arms behind my back. She started telling me a little more about this 100% nail polish, 95% dry, made AND distributed from New Jersey, USA. I liked what I heard – "no dry time, no smudges" with a "base coat, color coat, and top coat all in one" – then she showed me how easy they were to put on. Peel. Apply. Smooth right onto my nubby nails. I was amazed at how great these looked, even on me. Once I arrived home, I must have shown my husband fifty times while he was trying to watch football on television.

"Honey, did you see my nails?" "Hey, hon, can you believe these are my nails?"; "Hey honey, look, my nails sparkle!" And on and on and on.

My appointment with my medical massage therapist and this "twosie tester" would have me smiling from ear to ear on this same day. I forgot about everything else, including my MS. I was hyper-focused on nails; I felt like *I can do this.* I'm excited to tell my friends about what I found. Eager to learn more, I watched all the videos about the product, the company, and Fa Park's own "Never Give Up" story. His approach to creating this amazing product is similar to my Never Give Up approach to my life with multiple sclerosis. *I can do this. I want to do this.* I enrolled.

I became a Color Street Stylist even before I tried a full set. "*Feeling Marbelous*" was the first full Color Street Mani that I wore. My stomach dropped, but this time in a delightful way. Now my nails made me feel so good. *Dry Nail Polish, where have you been all my life?*

## ♫ "I'm So Excited" (The Pointer Sisters) ♫

Being a Color Street Stylist helps me feel relevant because I talk more and socialize with others. It provides a sense of belonging within our Color Street family as well. One afternoon, my friend Christine and I were brainstorming appropriate names for my website. Turns out the name we chose was inspired by the formerly my "Gnarly Nails," I used to hide. This new venture led me to gain confidence and believe in myself again. I can share Color Street's dry nail polish on my own schedule in small chunks of time. This is the best product and opportunity I never knew existed.

The following month, I learned about Color Street's foundation, which made nail sets for creating awareness and making charitable donations to various causes throughout the year. Interestingly, just weeks after I joined, the Foundation Donation set was Multiple Sclerosis Awareness. The nail set was called "Day by Day." Was it a coincidence, or just meant to be? I was still not ready to admit my own MS, so I instead announced that I was excited to purchase and wear this set in honor of my mother.

Being a Color Street stylist encouraged me to be visible and socialize after being in hiding for so long. And, thanks to Facebook, I could do this from my own home and on my own time. How different it was from the 1990s, when there were no cell phones or social media, and I lost so many connections after getting married and moving from West Virginia to Ohio. I recalled when in 2009, my dear friend Kim Branham Wilson called and said, "You need to get on Facebook now." *Wait, what is Facebook? Why do I need it?* It was like back in the '90s, when I couldn't understand why I needed a cell phone.

Thankfully, I hadn't resisted Facebook and had an online community; yet, in 2020, I still wasn't ready to share my MS with them.

Aryn was very aware and sensitive to my challenges with MS. One day she accompanied me to my neurologist appointment, then had to go directly to her waitressing job at Brennan's Fish House in Grand River. Her first available minute, she called me and, as she had so often lately, assumed the role of counselor.

"Mom," she insisted, "You are living your Best Life!"

After spending my adult life in a career centered on caring for others, I now had an opportunity to care for myself. The beginning physical issues of MS transferred over to take a mental toll on me. *I no longer fit in the world in the same way.* Fall of 2020 would be my first school year in over twenty-five years as an educator, that I would not be reporting for my first day back to school. On the first day, I cried. My husband and I talked it out. Although I was sad, I understood it was for the best. It felt strange not to plan my outfits for the week. My kids were adults. My son was working his internship. My daughter was in college. I now had the opportunity to focus on myself.

### Say What?

*Now what will I do?* In September 2020, I planned a priceless visit with my Aunt Sharon. She shared stories of her life, old letters from our relatives, and more stories of my mother. We also painted together. Aunt Sharon, who had painted decoratively for as long as I could remember, offered this advice: "Just paint what you see." We painted a picture of my favorite spot I would kayak to at the lake in our cove at Roaming Shores: the enormous willow tree with cascading leaves and branches. Aunt Sharon painted a chair for my mother. We felt Mom would have loved the tranquility of our cove at the lake. In the summertime, the sun would shine beautifully down our cove, and the fluffy white, billowing clouds would reflect off the water. In my kayak, paddling down the cove, past our neighbors' docks, seeing the perfectly imperfect lily pads so plentiful and floating in clusters. They were so beautiful as they bloomed with delicate, white flowers. Near the coastline, where trees may have fallen, the logs became a home to the turtles, perching all in a row. In a synchronized rhythm, they would dive off the log into the lake.

Slowly paddle further down the cove, and the resident blue heron might fly overhead, peacefully and gracefully gliding through the air surrounded by a gentle hug of the tall trees. I enjoyed looking up to gaze at the sun peeking through the leaves. I could breathe while kayaking on the lake. I painted with my aunt to capture my beautiful memories at the lake and, now, precious memories of us painting together.

In the following month, there were continued opportunities for growth and leadership within my Color Street family. Heather helped me uncover the next steps toward growth. "How do you feel about going 'live'?"

My response, "Absolutely not!"

These women helped by simply suggesting the ideas. By November 2020, I was feeling brave. I cried as I typed, admitting what I had kept hidden for so long. I shared my MS on my private "NoMoreGnarlyNails: Tips & Trends with Cheri" VIP Facebook group. With the support of this community, I was uncovering why Color Street was so important to me. It helped me to feel normal and stay connected. By January 2021, I was inspired to now share my MS on my regular Facebook page. I told them why I shared Color Street and my painting on my regular page. This was huge for me and quite scary. This was telling friends that I had not seen or spoken to in years about my private health issues. Next thing I knew, I was going "live." It was scary at first, but as I grew more confident and allowed myself to be vulnerable, I discovered that "I can" do it, and it felt good to connect with others.

## ♫ True Colors – (Cyndi Lauper) ♫

I was inspired to paint on my own, the Tree of Life. I felt ready to face my challenges and own them. It felt freeing. *"Be Amazing Every Day." Face it. Embrace it. Focus on Gratitude. Take Action. Achieve it. Believe it. With Peace and Love.* It's like following my own career lesson I used to teach my middle schoolers that I needed for myself.

## Vegas, Baby!

Scott's birthday was approaching in February. I asked, "Honey, what do you want to do for your birthday?" He replied, "Let's take a trip to Vegas." We had been researching the best areas to live in with low humidity. For me with my MS, low humidity feels better. – #1 Las Vegas, Nevada, and #6 St. George, Utah. I started to think and overthink the amount of walking. *I can bring my rolling carry-on with me through the airport to serve as a makeshift cane.* After all, people are walking with wheeled carry-ons while traveling. It reminded me of the scene in My Cousin Vinny, when Marisa Tomei said to Joe Pesci, "Oh, yeah, you blend." She was teasing him in the movie, but in my case, it was true!

At times, I can be headstrong, and my poor husband was trying to balance between my unspoken emotions of "I'm *tough*" and what I can *do for myself.* Then, without warning, I might switch and expect him to know when to step in and help me. We have since decided that the best way is what we used to say to our kids when they were preschoolers: "Use your words."

MS was mentally a struggle; you never really know how it will affect you from day to day, hour by hour, making it challenging for a planner like myself. Though I appeared "normal" on the outside, on the inside I might be exhausted beyond explanation, causing frustration and sometimes delayed responses that were difficult to navigate. On travel day, I had a fairly empty rolling carry-on as a walking assistant. I insisted on regular boarding and was not ready to accept the pre-board due to my disability. Once on the plane, as I lifted up my carry-on, a young man offered to help. I accepted. "Yes, thank you so much." The overhead compartments were getting full, and he was feeling the rush of people continuing to board the plane, so he handed my bag back to me. "Sorry, I tried." I appreciated the effort, but I really could have done without the next comment. Clueless. that my carry-on was really a "beard" to hide my need for a cane, he said, "That's what you get for not checking your bag."

Surprised by his snarky comment, I did not respond. What I want to say is, *I actually have MS and this is just my cane, and by the way, my bag IS checked.* Instead, my husband assisted and found a spot for my bag. I sat down, buckled my seatbelt, and got settled for take-off. And thought.

*How could he possibly know my struggles? I need to be real and quit trying to hide my challenges.* With MS, you may appear to be like everyone, which is a good, bad thing. This encounter was a lesson: *"Never hide your green hair," other people need to see it.* Angles Arrien's full quote can be found in *The Book of Awakening* by Mark Nepo. "Never hide your green hair. They can see it anyway." When I got home, I purchased my first fashionable cane, complete with flowers and engraved with my initials. The young man on the plane was trying to help. *How could he possibly know my struggles?*

On the way home from Las Vegas, we had a connecting flight in Denver. This connection strengthened my belief that things happen for a reason. Scott upgraded our tickets at the gate so we could get on the plane sooner. I was still not admitting to myself that I needed anything extra, but happy about Scott buying the upgraded early boarding; mentally, I was not ready to accept the "disabled" label.

That day on the plane, I met a new friend named Lucy who, as luck would have it, sat next to me. We chatted and connected because her daughter also has MS. I would not see Lucy again until December 2021. As a result of this trip, I learned to accept that I am not the same. *It's time to face it and embrace it.*

## Shenanigans?

In addition, my husband, the planner, had scheduled an appointment with a realtor. *I should have expected this as much as he was talking about it.* We had done the research and discovered that the climate in Las Vegas would actually be better for me since I am sensitive to humidity. At the hotel in Las Vegas, he'd showed me a list of a dozen houses in Mesquite and said we had an appointment on Wednesday with the realtors, and I needed to be ready to make a decision that day since the market was so very active. I told him I needed more time, so we drove about an hour to Mesquite, Nevada, to begin our self-guided tour and check out the area. As we drove along I-15 North, I was overtaken with emotion; the landscape was breathtaking. Snow-capped mountains were right out my window.

We had been driving for a while, and my eyes spontaneously began to tear up. *Where are we?* I asked Scott, and he replied, "We're here." We took the next exit and began to go down the list of twelve properties. For me, the first two were okay, followed by four in the same development that I automatically crossed off the list. This continued until we were at the last property. We got out of the car, and I told him that I liked the neighborhood, but this particular property was not the right spot for us. As we got back into the car, I could sense Scott's agitation. I buckled up, he started the car, then, with a forceful gesture, put it in drive. "Well, that's it," he said, "We're probably not going to get our winter house." As we looped around the cul-de-sac, I urged Scott to "*Stop!*"

The perfect house was for sale. I got out of the car to take a three-hundred-sixty-degree look around.

"This is my house," I said.

A couple of days later, we toured the houses and put in an offer on "my" house. It wasn't the newest one, but I knew it just felt right. We signed the paperwork and returned to Ohio while it was all processed – a reminder if Scott was talking about something, it may actually be in motion. Mesquite, Nevada, would be our new winter home.

# Chapter Nine
## *Standing*

In the spring of 2021, when I went to my six-month visit to my neurologist, she asked me what was different. My attitude was noticeably more positive. My happiness showed in my smile and demeanor as I entered her office. The difference was I was connecting and reconnecting with friends, learning to be open, sharing my challenges of MS, and feeling supported. My neurologist loved the effect being involved with Color Street has had on me – the positivity, my renewed confidence, the increased socialization, and the feeling of belonging – and she included my nail business in the report from my appointment. At first, I was scared of what people would think of me for no longer being an educator and now "selling" dry nail polish. It had started because I loved the product and needed to tell my friends all about it. I was so excited that I found this amazing dry nail polish. Then I discovered that being a stylist would be the perfect way to stay connected to my now former co-workers and old friends. The involvement continued with my personal growth and an opportunity to help others. Socialization and leadership opportunities fulfilled the needs that were missing in my life.

### Trash

Some people might be thinking, *Good for you, you are not reporting to work,* but when you are on a disability, it's a good/bad thing. Your paychecks are a fraction of what they once were. It seems backward to me that when you are on a disability, health insurance is lacking in coverage. My deductible is unreasonable. The out-of-pocket expenses to keep up with my MS would have the majority of my checks paying for my health care. They have increased that much; office visits can be five to twenty times more than I used to pay when I worked full-time. *I contributed for twenty-five years, and as long as I was working, my rates were good but, now that I am on disability, why is my insurance coverage terrible?* It's horrible. I get bills for thousands for my MRI to monitor the lesions of my brain and my neck. The costs can be more than I make in a month, and they did not even screen the lesions on my spine. The healthcare costs are so upsetting it can make a person like me question if they can even afford going to the doctor at all. I started deciding what medical recommendations I could put off; what I should do and what I would do become two different things because of the increased healthcare costs.

## ♫ "Ooh Ahh (My Life Be Like)" (Grits) ♫

My "I-cans of my fifties": I can meet new people. It was up to me to choose to respond and to take action. I was tired of hiding my issues, tired of the lost time. Scott and I planned to live in our new house in Mesquite, Nevada, during the winter months and in our condo in Fairport Harbor, Ohio, during spring and summer. I reflect back to the day of diagnosis back in August 2010 and wondering *whether* I would be walking five years out, ten years. *What was the expected timeline?* In 2021, I realized that the worry of being able to stand had been on my mind for years. I was happy to be fifty, relieved to reach this milestone because "I'm still standing."

## ♫ "I'm Still Standing" (Elton John) ♫

## Road Trip

In September 2021, Scott and I began the three-day, two-night road trip from Northeast Ohio to Mesquite, Nevada. Scott drove the entire time. Cosmo rode "shotgun." I put in my air pods and listened to Matthew McConaughey's book, *Greenlights*. It was delightful to listen to him tell his story for hours upon hours. Leo and I enjoyed the breeze from the window. Leo snuggled with me in the back row of the king cab of Scott's Ford Ranger while Matthew read to me. His distinct, sexy voice alone can make my knees buckle, "Alright, alright, alright, Greenlight!"

In Mesquite, we soon settled into new routines. I made friends during water aerobics at the recreation center. I enjoyed painting classes at the Fine Arts Association and hosting "Nail Gatherings" with my new friends. It was a great reason to get together, socialize, and do our nails. Life was good.

Soon, Scott and I were traveling again, this time to South Carolina for our son's graduation from bootcamp for the Army National Guard. I was anticipating the long walk through the Las Vegas airport, so that day I brought my cane. The sweet woman at the ticket counter greeted me with, "Good Morning!" She possessed a warm smile and, noticing my gait and my cane, said, "Can I call you a transport chair?"

*Oh boy, a transport chair? Um, I just don't know about this.*

I gulped. "How long is the walk?" Without hesitation, she picked up the phone, calling for a transport chair. Scott arrived from dropping me off at the door just as the transport chair arrived. This was the first time I had to admit that I actually needed help.

I tried not to make eye contact with people walking through the airport. I can stand and walk through the security area. I assume others must be thinking, *"You can stand, you can walk, then why aren't you walking to your gate?"* My head down shamefully, I passed through the security area.

We arrived early at the gate, and the attendant left the chair for me. I immediately got out of the chair and sat in the adjacent stationary seat. I was choked up as I called my Aunt Sharon. She answered the phone with a hello.

"Aunt Sharon?" I say with a lump in my throat, my quivering chin, and tears streaming uncontrollably down my cheeks.

"I used the transport chair to get through the airport."

I was worried that I had given up by accepting the chair. At first, I attempted to conceal my tears, but they continued to fall, making it impossible to hide. Since we had an hour or two before boarding, my husband's PHSD ("Post-Honeymoon Stress Disorder") was no joke and still lingered from our honeymoon airport experience. Seriously, we were always (and still are) the first ones at the gate, so I had plenty of time to reflect on the usefulness of the transport chair. While I was embarrassed, it allowed me to rest so I could say yes to other things. Talking to my aunt, hearing her voice, and listening to her thoughtful counsel helped me to recognize that it was okay to accept help.

My MS was so unpredictable, torture to a planner like me. I was at the mercy of my body. Each year, tasks continued to be just a little harder to manage. It was a little harder to walk, speak clearly, lift my legs, and use my hands; even digestion at times was exhausting. With unexpected changes hour by hour, day by day, year to year, I could hear my mom in my head sharing her struggles with MS: "If you don't use it, you lose it!"

## You're Being Selfish

I met Lucy for a reason. Remember, Lucy and I had sat next to each other on the plane from Las Vegas to Denver in February 2021. We would continue to message mostly about Lucy's daughter, Adrianne,

# 9 | STANDING

fellow MS warrior. Then Lucy and her husband Vinny invited Scott and me to their home for a delicious "dinner party." (For us, it was like having dinner with my "Uncle" Steve and "Aunt" Bernice Warcholak, cousins from Staten Island, New York.)

*It feels like Scott and I have known Lucy and Vinny for a lifetime.*

"You're being selfish," Vinny spoke the straight story. The lump formed in my throat, and my tears streamed. Lucy was so sweet; she held my hand, offering support as Vinny continued to explain that my family and I were missing out on life because I was not getting in the chair. This blows my mind; it's like a lightbulb has been turned on. This was exactly what I needed to hear to shift my thinking. The reality is that I have been the one keeping us stuck.

It was time to start seeking alternative ways of living my life. (By the way, I had asked Vinny for the straight talk after he told us about a conversation with Lucy's daughter.) This was a huge PIVOT. I'm thankful that Vinny was willing to have the tough talk, and Lucy was there to comfort me as the message was received. I am so grateful that Lucy and Vinny have entered my life for a reason and during this much-needed "season" of life. Gratitude for being my "family" and "being there for me."

As a result, I ordered a chair and requested a handicapped parking pass. It was humbling to admit that it was "time."

# Chapter Ten
## *Scared*

**Spring 2022**

In my master's degree program, I studied Maslow's Hierarchy, the Pyramid of Needs. I used to study the needs from the perspective of the child; now I was uncovering how my loss of career has affected me and my self-esteem. Not being an educator in the schools anymore was difficult. I needed to feel accomplished and help others. *What is my purpose?* I was scared, not sure where I belonged.

I reminded myself of my quote as an educator,

> **"In a gentle way, you can shake the world."**
> **– Mahatma Gandhi**

The quote on my Color Street pin: "Ask me how nail color can change lives." I had to admit that I used to roll my eyes at this pin. I was off-target with my original thoughts. Contrarily, the Color Street Foundation is a caring, generous, and charitable foundation committed to spreading awareness, making sizable donations to worthwhile causes. I am amazed and so proud to be a Color Street Stylist.

Reflecting on my daughter's essay written about my "meaningful life," I wanted to continue modeling a Never Give Up approach for myself and my family. I desired to make worthwhile contributions to the world. I pondered this thought for days before revealing my updated quote:

> "My mission in life is not merely to survive but to thrive: and to do so with some passion, some compassion, some humor, and some style."
> – Maya Angelou.

It was spring, and I was in Ohio to be near Aryn for lacrosse season. Scott and I have been living in the same household since 1994, never being apart for more than a few days. How were we going to manage to be apart through August? Now I was all alone until Aryn finished school, and it was a little scary. My heart was torn. My daughter was in Ohio but still at school. Scott, Alex, and the dogs were in Nevada. I was in Fairport, all alone. At this time, I was over fifty years old, and this was my first time living by myself. It was another opportunity to prove to myself that *I can*.

## ♫ "About Damn Time" (Lizzo) ♫

My solitude also gave me more time to think and reflect on my life, to figure my situation out, and find the inspiration for my dreams. I painted the mission statement by Maya Angelou. I hung it on the wall and repeated it daily, sometimes multiple times a day. I searched for inspiration. *What is my purpose? What am I doing? Is "observer" my new role in life?* No, I didn't think so. I felt like I had more to offer. I no longer worked in brick-and-mortar schools or taught fitness classes, but I was not willing to sit back and just be the spectator.

*What gives me another spark?* I bought another plaque to hang in my kitchen: "She remembered who she was, and the game changed." This quote by Clarissa Harlowe Barton was an awakening. Yes! Game on. I am someone. I have a master's degree. I am on a disability. I may not be rotating tires like in college, but I am still tough. I am resilient.

The ideas came rushing into my mind, touching my heart, pouring out of me and onto the pages rapidly. I reflected on the life my grandparents lived. They were so thoughtful and creative; they did not have the outside distractions of our modern world. More and more, I believed that my dad was right. It was important to sit with your thoughts to allow creative ideas to flood your brain. The peace and quiet are still so valuable. With no television or much distraction in my current living situation, it was time for me to reconnect with my roots and remember where I came from. I would begin connecting with nature. Stepping outside my front door, bare feet in the grass, grounding myself while peering out at the movement of the water of Lake Erie. It would draw me closer.

One sunny, unseasonably warm day in Ohio, I walked to our bank of mailboxes. Since Alex called from Nevada and we were still on the phone, I continued past the mailboxes. I left my cane in the condo because I did not intend to go far. I was aware that my gait was awkward, but I continued to push myself to go a little further. The sun was shining with a nice breeze coming off Lake Erie. Out of the corner of my eye I saw a woman walking her dog. Little did I realize at the time that she was also watching me. I walked a little further and paused. The woman with the leashed dog passed me.

"Excuse me, excuse me," I said as she turned and smiled.

"Your dog looks exactly like my dogs in Nevada," I told her. It was really uncanny, like it was like my dog sitting in front of me.

I later learned that she was wondering if she would need to intervene because I clearly was having trouble by the way I walked. We continued to walk together slowly, and we talked about my MS. We connected further because of her English accent. My sister-in-law, Janet Williams Warcholak, was originally from Liverpool, England. We talked more about her story of moving to the United States and, of course, the dogs. Her dog was a standard poodle too.

With the help of her daughter, Lindsie, we discovered that her standard poodle Archie was from the same litter as Leo, our second puppy. We are a "poodle family" owners of brothers. Archie's owner was Jane K. Jane and I exchanged numbers and began to meet regularly for fresh air, visits, and cuddles from Archie. After all, I needed a fur baby fix, being away from my boys, Cosmo and Leo, for the summer.

Jane was surprised that Archie felt so comfortable in our condo, taking treats and cuddling with me, Aryn, and Scott during his visits. She initially didn't think he would take a treat from me since he usually doesn't take treats from people he doesn't know. When they came over, we offered to get Archie water. Jane again didn't expect him to drink at our condo, but he drank. When Archie would see me, he was super-sweet and eager to greet me. *Could Archie remember us from when we met and he was a puppy?*

Meeting Jane and Archie was one of those precious synchronistic encounters in life. I did not plan to be walking where I was, and neither did Jane. Jane's poodle Archie is the perfect combination of Cosmo and Leo. Archie has the same parents as Cosmo, while Leo, Archie's littermate, has the same mom but a different dad. Small world, a natural combination, a dog family connection that was meant to be.

Later in June 2022, I was in a state of reflection and often jotted down my thoughts. I was also doing things I felt could help remedy my issues: I iced my feet because they tend to overheat, used my PEMF Pulsating Electromagnetic Frequency Health Wave Mat, and my Life Pro vibration plate to help with my circulation. My modified activity included a stationary bike, gentle yoga, and stretching with meditation. I needed to focus on what I could do.

## "I am willing to believe that things will always work out, even when they don't feel like it."

My story was flowing in my mind and in my dreams, quite literally waking me up in the middle of the night as times. I had to write and keep writing. Aryn moved into the condo with me for her summer break. While she was at her waitressing job, I flowed into writing routines. Aryn and I also established "roommate" routines together. Our mother-daughter summer was a gift of time.

The following month, Saturday, July 16, 2022, my daughter invited me to the Art Fest in Willoughby. Let's just say that invitations spark thoughts and overthinking. I pondered the invitation, wavered back and forth, tried to talk myself into going; I was tired of letting life pass me by. Aryn knew my sticking points, so we worked out a plan. I was hesitant but agreed to go.

Aryn and I were picking up her sweet friend, Sophia Hunter.

Aryn told me that Sophia's mom, Linda, was happy I was coming too, which made me feel so good. I told myself, *I can do it,* but my own insecurities crept in. I just moved at a different pace, a slower pace of which I was painfully aware.

When we arrived, I got out of the car at the stoplight with my cane, and then the girls drove farther to park the car. It felt wonderful to get out and to be social. I pushed myself to browse a few booths. In the past, shopping had been a favorite hobby. I used to go out for a day, buzzing from place to place. Now, the struggle was real.

It's scary and humbling to show up with my cane publicly. But the hugs as I was greeted by Linda Hunter, Stacey Smaretsky, and Sally Hunter let me know it was okay. I still belonged. They had been there for a while and were ready for lunch. I went with my "mom friends" to sit in the air-conditioned restaurant while Aryn and Sophia walked around the festival at their own pace, a pace much different from mine.

Sally and I have a dear friend in common, Nancy Archacki. So we decided we would have to send a selfie of us being together. It was these times, these moments, that made me pause and reflect. The once-normal everyday outings I used to take for granted now provided a shift to feeling *"I can."*

Sally was so cute; noticing my mani, she said, "I need that." Well, perfect! I put a Color Street Twosie tester on her right there at the table in the restaurant. It felt so good to see women smile and experience the joy of wearing Color Street's dry nail polish, to share some sparkle. This outing brought a feeling of belongingness, a feeling of normalcy l used to know.

## ♫ "This is How We Do It" (Montel Jordan) ♫

About 30 minutes later, Aryn came into the restaurant to get me. It was time for us to go home because she had to get ready for work. Hugs all around from these lovely women. Once on the sidewalk, still using my cane, Aryn offered me her arm for extra support and guidance through the crowd. She said, "You did good, Mom!"

She took a few selfies of us. Yay! I was smiling. I was genuinely happy to walk a couple of blocks, sit, socialize as I rested, and walk back to the car. This would never have been enough for me in the past.

Once we were back at the car, I had to lift my left leg with my arm because it had "crapped out." This short outing was a lot for me, but *I can. I did it!* It used to be easy to go out. I never had to think about how far I would have to walk or how long I would have to stand, or where I was going to find a bathroom. I just did events because I could. Be sure to enjoy the things you can do. For so long, I took so much that I was able to do for granted.

For me to say yes to attending the Art Fest was big. The courage to allow myself to be vulnerable, to "show my green hair" by taking my cane public.

When we arrived home, the hurt and cramping started to set into my legs and my hips. I laid down to rest and recuperate from the walk. For most, it wasn't far at all, but I started to feel the effects. The cane helped me regain some "I can" moments, but for a very limited time.

July 16, 2022 was my two-year anniversary of Color Street. It was the perfect day to recap my journey and celebrate how much my "No-MoreGnarlyNails" private Facebook VIP group means to me. On days when life was difficult, and I was quite fatigued, I could rest. I could sit and show ladies my current "nail situation" for any amount of time, even for a minute, based on how I felt. Being a stylist suits my needs. I love this community and the socialization. It's a community of belongingness. This community has made me feel so good.

## Punched in the Gut

The next morning, I slipped out of the condo while Aryn was still asleep to get coffee. As I drove down the street toward the stop sign, I saw it: The 2022 Pirate Triathlon. Thoughts immediately entered my mind as short memory clips. It was like déjà vu, but I *knew* I had been here before. I recognized the orange cones, the park rangers, the police, the bikes, and the runners. It was like a punch in the gut. The last time I attended this event was as a competitor, along with my friends, in 2009.

I was on the phone with my friend Christine. I was overtaken by emotion seeing the racers, and tears began to stream down my face, mourning the life that I once loved, literally running right past me. I was shocked that I was crying. It had been so long. My life had evolved. This life of a triathlete was unrecognizable in my world today. My tears cleansed my soul and helped me release that chapter of my life. It was like I was meant to experience this event so I could mourn the loss and let it go. *Intense.*

I pivot to reflect on the gift of MS. The gift to slow down. If I were not dealing with the challenges of MS I would not experience life in the way I do today. I returned home to the condo, and I "feel the feels" all over again. My "NoMoreGnarlyNails" VIP community was responding to my social media story from yesterday. I was comforted by them – family and friends – some from high school, others from college, from my career in education, and from new chapters of my life with Color Street, friends from Nevada, and friends I'd never met in person and would like to hug one day. I was learning to be open, to be vulnerable.

In August, I plan to attend the National Color Street Conference in Phoenix, Arizona. I booked my ADA (Americans with Disabilities) room at the Hyatt. My dear friend Christine, who was attending too, said, "Whatever you need, I'm there." I told her she did not need to feel responsible for caring for me. I set a goal to buy myself a Kate Spade Tote and purse for the Color Street conference. Instead, I chose the more practical "Steve Madden" backpack from my favorite store, T.J. Maxx; I also purchased myself a "senior mobility-walker/transport chair" in sky blue. It pissed me off that it is labeled "senior" and that the photos are all of seniors. Where are the people that looked like me?

When my kids were growing up, I bought a plaque that read, "Be STRONG enough to stand alone, SMART enough to know when you need help, and BRAVE enough to ask for it." I now realize that plaque is for me. I decided on a daily checklist, just for me; checking off accomplishments helps me feel better, being a checklist person.

## My 5-Step Daily Checklist

**Move:** My movement certainly is not the same 3-5 miles I used to run on the treadmill before work. Instead, it's getting out of bed, making the bed, doing a little gentle yoga, stretching, using hand weights, swimming or riding a stationary bike, and showering (which also takes energy to do.)

**Hydration & Nutrition:** I can drink water. I can continue to take my Juice Plus+ whole food supplement, along with the omegas and other recommended supplements.

**Connect:** I can socialize. I can use text and Messenger.

I let others know I am thinking of them. Often I just don't have the energy or the stamina for a conversation.

**Take Action:** Every day, I do something to feel productive. I can do my own nails (thanks to Color Street), share tips with the team, and my VIPs. I can do daily chores. I get the mail at the mailbox, wash the dishes or load/unload the dishwasher, and take care of the laundry. Additionally, I can work on an activity I enjoy, like writing or editing, painting, scrapbooking, reading or listening to books.

**Self-Care:** I can self-massage fascia that builds up in my body or schedule a massage. I stand on my vibe plate to help with circulation.

I can follow Trevor Wicken on Instagram and consider joining "The MS GYM" online program, recommended by a friend, sorority sister, and fellow MS Warrior. I can get dressed (It's hard to believe that I actually have this on my list, but it does take effort.) I do my hair sometimes (at times, my left hand doesn't work well enough to use an elastic for a messy bun. The '80s-style scrunchies work better when that happens.) Applying my makeup takes effort as well (goals for a glam quad, one day.)

I try to wash some healthy options ahead of time, so I have ready-to-eat snacks. This could use some improvement.

I think of my mom and the things she would tell me. Much like her, I believe I am one of the lucky ones. I did get to enjoy a "normal" childhood and young adult life. I practice a mindful moment of gratitude. I reread or listen to "The Man in the Arena" speech that Brené Brown introduced me to in her Netflix special, *The Call to Courage*. I also regularly review my goals on my vision board.

I can also listen to my body and choose to allow myself to rest. I set a timer so I don't lose track of time.

> *Write your own list:*
>
> *Check off the things that you do for your own personal wellness and wins for the day. Start with small, manageable goals and check them off.*

## Moving

In the blink of an eye, it was August, and yet again, new plans would evolve. My time residing in Ohio would be coming to an end. The condo had sold, and my hubby arrived at Fairport Harbor to help load the furniture and belongings from it. Soon I would join him and Alex full-time in Nevada. In the meantime, movers were moving Aryn into her college house as she was resuming classes, and I was preparing for my trip to Phoenix.

The Color Street Conference was a big goal, given my mobility issues. I bought and used the walker that transformed into a transport chair. *Thank you, Christine, for pushing me from our hotel to the conference and down to the pool so I could conserve my energy for the informational sessions. Thanks to all the amazing women, new friends* who never hesitated to help when Christine and I attended different sessions. During breaks, I took breaks. I would sneak naps back in the room. I just paced myself. Life was continuing to change.

Becoming a Color Street Stylist was like entering a sisterhood. This opportunity entered my life for a reason. Jen McCann, rock star stylist, receives award after award. I am thirteen levels below her, but I feel seen. She truly knows how to make a girl feel special. She texts. Jen had saved me and Christine a seat at her table for dinner on Saturday evening. This kindness "fills my cup" with a feeling of real belongingness. Fa Park, founder and creator of Color Street, sits just two tables away with his family. Woo-hoo! I can conference. *I belong. Check.*

Once back in Nevada, I reflected on my accomplishments. It felt good to be social at the Color Street conference. On September 22, 2022, I should have been going on a trip to Mexico that I earned with Color Street. I declined the trip, not fully confident in my independence. One of my goals is to become physically stronger so I can go on future company trips.

## Do You See Me?

I was determined to find another way. After watching the documentary *Introducing Selma Blair,* I felt a renewed eagerness to stop hiding and be seen, to be part of life again. Selma Blair found another way and made a lasting impression on my life by sharing her story. She is an MS Warrior, actress, and advocate. Tired of missing out on life, I too was ready to face the challenge. After watching Selma using her Alinker, I ordered one, my very own walking bike, to improve my strength, become more active, and move more independently.

It arrived just in time, hours before we were to meet our friends, Louanne and Aric Albrio, who were in Vegas from Connecticut. Now, these aren't just any friends – they had become very dear to us over the years. It was a connection that never would have happened had I not been open to meeting Scott's high school girlfriend. I loved how Louanne described us (me and her) by saying, "Scott has good taste." I describe Scott and Louanne like Jerry and Elaine from *Seinfeld*.

The four of us enjoyed a fantastic evening in downtown Las Vegas. With my Alinker, I felt like "me" again, a social butterfly. Tonight I was seen. I was using the Alinker for the first time, and it provided me with more stability, more stamina, and more independence. People were talking to me and approached us; they were curious and wanted to know more about my "walking bike."

The Alinker changed the way others look at me and how I see myself in the world. *It's freeing!* Prior to using the Alinker, I felt limited. Now, I was once again excited for future outings, to go to parks and on walking trails, and maybe *I can* bring the dogs too. I CAN go to the mall and take trips. I plan to attend YSU's women's lacrosse games in Ohio. Additionally, I plan to visit friends and family, making stops in West Virginia, Pennsylvania, and Maryland. I plan to visit my brother in Florida. I feel like I can plan a visit to my "other brother" in Germany (Future Goals). What has changed is my belief in myself. I can too! Using the Alinker has opened my mind. The world has just become accessible to me – I feel like I belong in it!

Most smile and speak to me; now I'm at eye level. Some even share words of encouragement. When I was using a cane, walker, or wheelchair, I often felt unseen. I noticed myself looking down. Now I can look up and face the world.

As my husband and I strolled down the LINQ promenade in Las Vegas on the eve of New Year's Eve, an adorable woman excitedly ran over to me. "Is that an Alinker?" she asked. When I said yes, she introduced herself as Annabelle and then told me of her friend – a former marathon runner and MS Warrior in South Africa – who also used the Alinker. Annabelle hugged me and asked to get a picture together for her friend. The Alinker had made me approachable and helped me meet new friends around the world, like Annabelle from Dubai. I wish I had asked her to send me the picture. Meeting Annabelle was delightful and made my day; I hope we will meet again.

My quote was becoming my reality. Maslow's Hierarchy: the pyramid of needs; these needs are being fulfilled by the Alinker, by sharing Color Street, and feeling support from friends, family, and fellow MS warriors. My life has manifested from my quote and my openness to a new vision, a belief in myself.

*I can.* I am ready to take action by sharing my story, to Never Give Up. There are a lot of symptoms, frustration, and an increasing weakness which has been challenging to navigate with MS, the unknowns. For me, it was the quiet reflection and thinking that brought clarity. The solitude has been so thought-provoking. I believe. I Pivot in reflection and revisit my quote as an educator:

> **"In a gentle way, you can change the world."**
> **–Mahatma Gandhi**

The time has come to Pause, to Breathe, and to reveal where the "Pivot" all began back in January 1990. Hang on, let me get my tissues, then join me for the first ride that sparked my unforgettable journey.

# PART III
# Pivot

# Chapter Eleven
## *Unraveled*

My beautiful blond-haired, blue-eyed sister was living life to the fullest. An avid reader, incredible student, and fun sorority sister, she possessed that "get it done" drive and was graduating early with her degree in elementary education. Why was Beth so motivated to get college completed early? She was engaged to her college sweetheart with plans to be married in August 1990. She had already accepted a full-time teaching position to begin her career in the city where her fiancé resided. Seriously, the girl was living right. Who else could land a full-time teaching job mid-school year? At the age of twenty-one, Beth's plans were falling right into place.

It was the weekend before Beth was to start her new life, with a new career, a new apartment, a new story to create. Mom and I were traveling from Fairmont to support her in the new beginnings. We wanted to be sure she was settling into her apartment in a small town near Martinsburg. Much like Beth, I was involved in my freshman year of college with Greek life and quickly bonded to my Sigma, Sigma, Sigma pledge sisters. And like Beth, I had a plan.

My plan was to complete my general studies at Fairmont State College, our hometown college, then transfer to pursue a degree in Physical Therapy.

My plan was in place. I was checking off the boxes one at a time: college, sorority and social life, boyfriend, and the beginnings of my modeling portfolio. Life was good and happening according to plan.

On Friday, I shadowed Beth's future sister-in-law, Donna Lyons, a physical therapist for the schools. I was checking off my to-do list. Freshman year shadowing experience, check. The shadowing experience was amazing. I thoroughly enjoyed all components of the job; the intellectual, the physical, and the social interaction of this career as a physical therapist. *This path feels right. This career suits me perfectly. This plan, my plan, is working out.*

Later that evening, the three of us talked, laughed, cried, and enjoyed each other's company. Beth's life was on course. Her apartment was in order, and the plan was in place. The following morning, brunch was on the schedule. We would meet Beth's in-laws before departing. We settled in for a good night's sleep, never imagining that this would be the last time we slept peacefully under the same roof.

The following morning, we woke up refreshed and checked our plan for the day. Getting ready to go out anywhere was just something I did. My big eighties hair was teased perfectly in place, my make-up trending with black eyeliner on the inside of my lower lash line. I'm not really sure that it was a great idea to line the inside of my eyelid with a cheap eyeliner pencil. I am questioning that decision, but my outfit was definitely on-point for a casual brunch.

I was so excited as I removed the tags from my new pants, purchased just the week before at Casual Corner, that would make their first public appearance at brunch. I loved the deep teal color of my brand-new high-waisted pleated linen pants. I slipped them on, adding a soft, medium brown belt with cream-colored threading. I then laced up brown leather ankle-high booties with chunky, slouching teal-colored socks that coordinated perfectly. I was delighted.

I would shift the style of my outfit to a casual appearance by sliding into a bold, multi-colored patchwork, fluffy ski jacket. It made a bright, bold "look at me" statement that said, "college student on the go; fun and fashionable with a flair." Beth would characterize me as the

Fashionista of the family. Truth be told, I think it drove her a little crazy with me styling my outfits and primping so much. I know she thought it was excessive. But it was my thing. It brought me joy. I liked the attention. I was tall, thin, and often asked if I modeled. My thought: you just never know who you are going to meet when you are out. There was no Instagram, no Snapchat, and no Facebook, so you just had to be ready at all times. Going out anywhere was your exposure.

My mom shared with us the advice that she and Aunt Sharon received from their mom, our beloved Granny. I can almost hear the words coming out of her mouth. Mom would share Granny's advice in a whisper:

"Always be sure you are wearing clean panties when you leave the house."

When we giggled at this advice, she would add, "You never know." So true; you never know. What happened that day would not only leave us with broken bones and scars on our bodies but in our hearts forever.

We proceeded to brunch. It was clear that Beth was part of a warm and loving family that was not only welcoming her with wide open arms but me and Mom as well. We were greeted with kind, smiling eyes and warm, genuine hugs. It was a lovely brunch, and the feeling of calm washed over me. I felt confident that my sister Beth was following her path, her plan. She was exactly where she needed to be.

Nearing the end of brunch, as I peered out the window, I could easily see the weather conditions changing. Mom and I looked at each other from across the table with some concern. We had better get moving if we were going to make it through the mountains and home before dark. The second semester of college classes resumed for me on Monday.

Smiles and hugs were all around as we departed from Beth's in-laws following brunch. That light-hearted feeling lasted until we opened the door and the cold, brisk air took our breath away. We surveyed the conditions. Our plan for the rest of today began to feel more daunting and task-oriented. We rushed into the car to escape the elements.

The plan: get back to Beth's apartment, change, pack quickly, and start driving. *I can't get stuck in this town. I have to get back for class. My plan resumes Monday.* We fell quiet, and a serious tone resonated in the car.

At this point, the roads and the weather conditions were becoming increasingly dangerous. Beth was in the driver's seat and Mom in the front, both securely fastened with their seatbelts. I was sitting in the middle of the backseat.

What began as a fun weekend of checking off boxes continued with big, beautiful, white fluffy snowflakes would quickly transform into slush, sliding, wrecks, grunts, broken bones, and broken hearts. Definitely mine.

*But what about my plan?*

*Pause. Breathe.*

# Chapter Twelve
## Crushed

**January 8, 1990**

There was an eerie kind of quiet as we drove out of the city limits toward Beth's apartment. You could feel the tires struggling to grip the road as we rounded a corner and crest the top of the hill. The visibility was steadily decreasing as the snow continued to fall more quickly. You could see there were just a few houses and fields ahead in the distance. We were in a sparsely populated area, and no cars were in sight, which was good because of what happened next.

I grabbed the handles on each of the doors in the backseat in our car. First sliding sideways, then rotating and spinning like a top gaining momentum as we were whisked down the hill and continuously spinning out of control. It was the kind of feeling like you have been launched off a merry-go-round or like the video game *Mario Kart* when you hit the banana peel. The noise from skidding through the slush came to an abrupt halt as we forcefully dropped vertically over an embankment on the opposite side of the road. We were at rest. *Pause. Breathe.*

Snow, muck, and branches pressed against the driver's side windows. *Is everyone okay?* The car rested on its side with tires off the ground. *Now what?* In 1990, we did not have cell phones at our fingertips. We looked around and could see a small house in the distance.

I was so annoyed. This situation was just *not* part of the plan. Beth was trapped in the driver's seat, down low near the brush. The ground pressed against the window, which was thankfully still intact. I was concerned that our car could topple over onto the roof. Our sweet mom was dangling in the air, being held in only by her seatbelt. We decided I would go search for a phone to call for help.

The Plan: Find a Phone. Call for a tow truck to pull us out quickly. We need to get on the road. *I'm not getting stuck in this town.*

It was a struggle to open the door against gravity. I stood and jumped upwards, pushing, pulling, and lifting myself up to get out of the car. It felt like I was climbing straight up and out of a submarine. I am out of the car. *Pause. Breathe.*

Since I didn't anticipate any further issues and my adrenaline was pumping, I didn't even notice the cold, though huge flakes continued to fall. I swiftly jogged on the berm of the road to the nearest house, leaving my family behind. I was in task-oriented, checklist mode. I did not even think of grabbing my jacket, a decision I would later regret. My plan was to knock on the door, get help, and quickly return. A tow truck would be called. Mom and I would experience a minor delay in our return trip. We would be back on track with the plan. I was certain Mom and I could still be home before sunset.

The wind gust, the cold air engulfed me. At this point, I was thinking, *I should have grabbed my coat.* I hopped up the stairs onto the porch quickly, rubbed my cold hands together, and assessed the house. Thin slats of white-painted wooden siding were peeling and exposing bare spots of natural wood. The small house was desperately in need of attention, a fixer-upper. It was quiet, dark inside, and just looked like a lonely place to live. *I would not want to live here.* I knocked, no answer. I knocked more vigorously this time, but still no answer; no lights came on. I began to anxiously pace the length of the porch, hoping to get a response. *Come on. Come on. Is anyone here? It's quiet. And I am alone.*

I walked to the side of the rundown porch and leaned over the loose banister to peer down the snow-covered gravel driveway. There was no garage and no cars in the driveway. *Now what?* In the distance, I faintly recognized the sounds of a door shutting, which grabbed my attention. I snapped my head back toward the car where Beth and Mom were stuck. A large truck had stopped to assist! As I got closer, I noticed the medium gray color, and I felt the heat blowing from inside the truck as I approached his open window. This man has stopped to help us.

Our revised plan was in motion. *Check.*

Even while sitting in his truck, it was clear he was a big, rugged man who was prepared for such situations. He was a doer, not a talker, a strong, quiet type with an unspoken air of "I got this." The flares were out, his headlights were on, and his hazard lights were flashing with caution. The area feels secure, protected.

The weather conditions had worsened. It was challenging to see through the blowing snow. I had to squint to prevent the snowflakes from colliding with my eyes. As he got out of his truck, I felt a sense of calm, like it was going to be okay because help had arrived. I allowed myself to sigh.

"Is everyone okay?" he asks.

We were fine, but my mom had MS, and my sister and I were having trouble coming up with a plan to safely get her out of the car. Mom's MS was progressive, so every year life was just a little harder, and she was not quite able to keep up. Meanwhile, I was distracted by the unsteadiness of the car, smashed against the brush. *Could the car continue to roll down the hill?*

Two more cars cautiously approached the scene and offered assistance. You gotta love good ol' West Virginia boys. No matter the age, they are always tough and ready to help. *Yes, we can. We can fix this.* More help had arrived.

One gentleman was traveling by himself, and the other had a full car of people. The full car was parked on the opposite side of the road. I saw the rubberneckers in the back seat staring at us from the rear window, trying to get a glimpse of what had happened. With the assistance of the kind men in that small town, we were able to get both Mom and Beth safely out of the car. And then, in the blink of an eye, it all changed. The peaceful feeling of relief that Mom was safely out of the car turned abruptly to terror.

From there, everything happened both quickly and in slow motion. The giant metal beast (I can best describe it as a Hummer in sedan form), sliding in our direction with locked tires, rapidly bearing down on us. My chest tightened with panic. My eyes widened while the metal beast shortened the distance between us.

Chaos, confusion, and panic erupted as Beth and I did not hesitate to protect our mother. She urged us to run ahead. "*Just go, run!*" Her selflessness was real, but there was absolutely no chance we would separate from her. Beth and I refused her plea without so much as a word. We just secured our protective grip, almost in unison, taking our mother's hand and holding her arm to help steady her.

The scene intensified; voices could be heard yelling, and bodies could be seen running in a desperate attempt to get out of the way. The sounds I heard were the scuffles of Mom doing her best to move her feet, shuffling through the gravel on the berm. Her struggle, our struggle, was real.

Beth was at Mom's left side. I was on her right. We scampered as quickly as possible down the side of the road. One man has traveled back toward his truck for protection. Another man crosses the road to return to his car. There was one man leading the way right in front of me. At this point, we were all in this together. I heard the car skidding, the overwhelming whoosh, and then we were violently overtaken.

The moment before impact, I recall twisting my torso to try to see how close the danger was. The beast was practically on top of us. There was nowhere for us to go. I recall a kind of take-your-breath-away grunt as the three of us absorbed the impact.

The momentum threw me up and over the beast to, thankfully, land in the snow-covered grass. My mom and sister were forcefully dragged against their will over the hill. The hardened, frozen ground did not offer any cushion. My mom and sister were sucked into the abyss of that automobile.

This was not part of my plan! And then, it was quiet.

*Pause. Breathe.*

## Chapter Thirteen
# R.I.P.

There was a chilling silence, with only the muffled sounds coming from the gusting wind on that stormy Saturday, January 8, 1990. There I was, an eighteen-year-old college student, lying on the frozen, snow-covered ground alone, in shock and utter disbelief at what had just happened.

I had been awakened by her screams. That voice, I recognized it. It sounded familiar, much like the one that had provided me with love and support throughout my life, but it was now filled with panic and distress. Mom was crying out for me. It was the kind of scream that sends shivers down your spine. She was stuck. The metal beast had her pinned against the frozen earth. The only thing she had was her voice.

Where was I? On the hill beyond her reach, beyond her sight. In the distance below, through the grass and snow-covered brush, I saw the top of my mother's head and her shoulders protruding from under the metal beast in the distance. I saw her dark hair and her bright red pea-coat. I heard her, but she was so terribly far away, unreachable.

I attempted to reply, but I had no words. I couldn't make a sound. Even if I could, I doubt she would have been able to hear me.

After becoming a mother myself, those screams took on a whole new meaning. I understood the willingness to do anything, even sacrificing one's own life, for their children. My mother must have felt so helpless lying trapped underneath that metal beast, unable to help her daughters.

Beth was next to her. Her back was to me as she was facing the car. I was puzzled. I later learned that my dear sister had been dragged down the snow-covered hill on her knees, connected only by her hair and somehow attached to the front wheel well. Seriously, her hair was entangled and attached to the beast. *Why was this happening?*

*Pause. Breathe.*

An older gentleman came to check on me. He had thick, wavy, and wiry silver hair and wore a plaid quilted flannel complete with triangle, pointed flaps, and cream-marbled swirl snaps. As he slowly approached, I could sense his gentle presence. He knelt down close to me and looked into my eyes, forging a connection that touched my soul and my thankful heart. He was with me for a reason.

This older gentleman had the most beautiful crystal blue eyes, the kind I had only seen on one other beautiful soul: my granny. I was mesmerized by his eyes. Simply by a look, he held me in a place of calm amidst the chaos. And then he spoke to me and said something that my granny likely would have said,

"Honey," he said softly, "I think you have a little broken leg."

I didn't make a sound, but in my head, I was vigorously responding, *No shit!*

Adrenaline rushed through my body from the shock. I remember the heat, even though there was snow all around. My femur bone was clearly snapped in two. Instinctually, I forcefully pressed my shattered femur bone back where it belonged, back into my quadricep. Each time I moved, I willed it to stay in place, but it continued to jut out again and again. Note: my femur bone was snapped, protruding at a ninety-degree angle, but thankfully, it did NOT break through the skin. I doubt I would have been so calm if I was covered in blood. My thought was, *I could just push my bone back in place, if only it would stay in my leg where it belonged.* I finally responded to the man with the eyes that reminded me of Granny who, under different circumstances, would be happy to know that my "panties are clean" today.

I pleaded with the man. *Will you please just go to my mother? Will you tell her I'm okay?*

The combination of the nip in the air and the frozen ground began to chill me to the bone. Then I saw the flashing lights of the rescue squad. I heard doors opening and then slamming shut. The EMTs on the scene began to assess the situation. As the snow continued to fall, the locals stayed to direct the EMTs to ensure our safe transport.

There was shouting, and judging from their voices, they were not much older than me. "Call another ambulance!" The first young EMT slipped and skidded quickly down the hill to assess me. He yelled to his co-worker, "Bring the stretcher!" Worried for my mom and my sister, I asked about them. He explained that they would be taking me first, then my mother and my sister last, based on the injuries. *What were their injuries?*

There were so many unanswered questions as I lay on the snow-covered ground in my cute teal high-waisted pleated pants. Unfortunately, my coat was still in the car. *This was a waste of my fun and fashionable outfit.* Then the EMT announced the worst news *ever!* He pulled out what I recall as an enormous pair of ... *scissors.* For me, an avowed fashionista and shopaholic, I was appalled. How dare he think he was coming anywhere near my pants with *those scissors!*

*"Please,"* I pleaded in an attempt to persuade him to see things my way, *"I just bought these last week."* I mean, seriously, I had just taken the tags off that day. There had to be another way.

I'm certain he was like:

*You are Insane! Like, what the hell is wrong with you, your precious pants? Really? Wake up. Ummm, hello, your bone is shattered into pieces! Your skin is all that is holding your bones together, and you are begging me to save your pants???*

Of course, he didn't say any of this to me (though I'm certain he retold this story later over beers to his buddies). He just calmly and patiently explained to me that there was, in fact, no other way. Then, as the snow continued to cover us, the scissors reappeared. Just like that, he sliced my cute teal high-waisted pleated linen pants from the bottom near my right ankle all the way up to my belt. Sheer disappointment washed over me as I lay back on the cold, hard, snow-covered wooden stretcher.

Now it was time for him and the other EMTs to climb back up the embankment while carrying the stretcher. The struggle was real, and I was painfully aware there was nothing I could do to help. I was deadweight, able only to grip the sides of the stretcher as the EMTs tried to maintain their own footing while climbing up the slippery slope. Just picture it. Me, the fashionista on the stretcher with one pant leg on and one pant leg cut off. A total fashion emergency. So sad, so scared, so very alone.

*Please join me for a moment of silence…*

*R.I.P. to my adorable, deep teal, high-waisted, pleated linen pants.*

## 13 | R.I.P.

Finally, I was in the ambulance. The lights and sirens were turned on, and the doors closed so we could depart for the hospital. Thankfully the second squad had just arrived, and that group of EMTs quickly moved into action, heading down the slippery slope to attend to my mother and sister, who were still attached to "the metal beast." The EMTs assured me that everything would be okay and I would see my mom and my sister at the hospital.

Everything was out of my control. I was alive, yet broken. My mom and my sister were alive but injured, and to what degree, I just don't know.

*My new favorite pants have been destroyed. My plans are wrecked. What about my classes on Monday?*

*Pause. Breathe.*

# Chapter Fourteen

## *Goodbye*

The EMT in the back with me yelled forcefully at the driver of the squad to *slow down*. We were sliding! I felt he was refraining from what he really wanted to yell. There was panic in their voices as the roads remained treacherous.

My mom always used to say that people come into your lives for a reason, a season, or a lifetime. I would never again see the sweet old man with the crystal blue eyes, the gentleman who so kindly stopped to help put out flares, or the other kind citizens of that small town who didn't hesitate to step in and assist while risking their own safety. Thank you to each and every one of you.

And to the unknown driver of the metal beast, who I never properly met but impacted my life so dramatically: I would never wish the nightmare of being behind the wheel on that snowy January day on anyone. I'm so sorry for the thoughts that must still haunt you at the sign of inclement weather. I forgive you. It wasn't your fault.

Instead, what I would like to let you know is that although "The Accident," as we referred to it, changed the course of my life, it ultimately made me a better person. If you haven't yet found forgiveness for yourself in your heart, I hope that allows you to do so.

Last but not least, I would also like to express my gratitude to the EMTs that were there for a *reason*. I am grateful for your help, even to the EMT with the damn scissors that cut off my cute teal pants. I forgive you too.

*Pause. Breathe.*

# Chapter Fifteen

## *Alone*

*L*ater that same snowy Saturday night, I woke up disoriented and lonely in a dimly-lit hospital room with strangers in my room. *What the hell? Why is there a huge bolt protruding out from either side of my shin? I'm stuck! Where is my mom? My sister? Can somebody help me?*

Suddenly, two kids dash into the room and rush past me to the woman in the other bed. As they do, I feel agonizing pain, as well as a great deal of confusion. *Wait, what is that?! Why did it hurt as they went past?*

I pushed the call button, and the nurse entered several minutes later.

"Hi, I'm Shirley. It is nice to see you are awake. How are you doing?"

I just looked at her with a blank stare. *Really? How do you think I'm doing? Hello, I'm the one that just got run over by the huge car.*

Shirley began to explain the contraption attached to my body. "So this pulley system is connected to you with weights hanging over the edge of your bed. It's attached with this bolt through your shin. There are weights hanging over the end of the bed." She paused. "I'm gonna go get one of those bright yellow caution signs the janitor uses when he's mopping so the kids quit bumping into the weights."

*Mystery solved. Yes, a sign is a great idea.* In the meantime, I will hold my breath and shudder each time the kids pass.

The weights attached to a rope, secured to the bolt sticking out of my shin, attached to my fragmented broken bone, my femur bone, my poor femur bone. *Please hurry. Get the sign. In and out, back and forth, the kids rush past my hospital bed.*

"And what about my mom and sister," I asked.

"Oh, the hospital is overcrowded," Shirley said, "so they are on the eighth floor, the maternity floor. You are on the fifth floor, for surgery. It's scheduled first thing Monday morning."

*Oh great.* I think sarcastically, *surgery… wait! Monday? My second semester of class starts on Monday.*

The nurse continued to hurry around the room – writing her name on the white wipe-off board and filling a cup of water for me while explaining that the weights were helping my muscles settle into place to prepare for surgery.

"Your sister will be released on Monday, and you get to take her spot in the maternity ward with your mother. One more thing: the weather is so bad that your dad won't be here until mid-week." My head is spinning. Information overload. *Mid-week? Here? What about my classes? I have to get back to Fairmont.* Reality is starting to set in. I'm stuck. I think about my schedule, my plans. I wish I was with my mother. The nurse leaves the room, and again I am alone.

*Pause. Breathe.*

While drugged up on pain meds and struggling to move, I managed to pick up the receiver of the phone and dial. Somehow, I remembered the home phone number of my boyfriend. He was still in Pennsylvania on winter break. I composed myself as much as possible, trying to pretend I was just making a regular phone call.

*Please be home; please be home to take my call. I'm all alone.*

### ♫ "Lonely" (Akon) ♫

In 1990, you dialed landlines. It was our only option. I crossed my fingers, hoping that someone would answer the ringing phone and that Jeff would be available to come to the stationary phone. I knew exactly where it was attached to the wall since I had just recently visited.

Thankfully, his mother picked up.

"May I please speak to Jeff?" I asked softly. Did she think this was odd, being that I'd just been there a few days ago? Maybe, but it was all I could muster the strength to say.

His mother called to him, then, after a couple of minutes, I heard Jeff's voice on the other end.

Jeff?" I said, my voice cracking. That's when I began to crumble. I broke down in a muffled sob, trying to control myself. These were the first tears I had shed from this event that had upended my life.

I tried to speak quietly as the woman in the bed next to me, her husband, and two kids, were separated by just a thin hospital curtain, but it was just too much. I was completely overcome with emotion, and my poor boyfriend was blindsided. His fashionista, "put together" girlfriend with a get-it-done checklist was unraveling.

I recall the concern in his voice as he desperately tried to figure out what had happened to me and where I was. "Wait," he said gently,

"Calm down; try to quit crying." When this didn't work, he paused and tried again. "Hon, I can't understand you."

And again, I'm all alone.

*Pause. Breathe.*

# Chapter Sixteen
# *Interrogated*

After surgery, I couldn't wait to see my mom in our shared hospital room on the maternity floor. I was wheeled down the hall in a hospital bed that was tall and equipped with a metal bar across the top. A chain-link kind of rope hung down with a triangle bar suspended in the air for me to hold onto to lift or reposition myself. Little did I know that I would not be getting out of bed for over a month or that the room would become my home for a season.

My first impression was that it was nice and bright; the curtains were open, and the sun was shining through the large picture window. *Oh yay!* As it turned out, it was a nice view of the parking lot. *Ugh!*

I was expecting to be greeted, seeing Mom's beautiful smile and hearing her voice say, "Hi, honey. I'm so happy to see you!" The delightful anticipation gave me a feeling of comfort. Oh how I just wanted to go to her, curl up in her twin hospital bed with her, have her wrap her arms around me and tell me that everything was going to be okay. Instead, I found the room empty and that I was to remain attached to my bed. That's when the nurse informed me that Mom was in surgery.

*Wait – what?!*

Remember, I was down on the fifth floor with no clue about what was happening to my mom and sister. The nurse then told me her name was Carla and that Mom should be up in an hour or so.

Carla's scrubs were burgundy colored with a v-neckline. She wore her long, brown hair in a ponytail. It was so thick. *I bet she could only loop an elastic around her hair twice.*

As she spoke, I could tell from her voice and her big beautiful smile that she truly enjoyed her job.

"We usually only get ladies for a couple days," she said, reminding me we're in the maternity ward. "Looks like you and your mom will be with us for a while."

Her back is to me, so she cannot see my grimace. *Great!*

Unanswered questions play on repeat: *Why am I still attached to my bed? What is this bolt still doing in my shin with the pulley system and the weights still attached to me? I already had surgery. I should really be in class this morning.*

Carla then told me the surgeon would be in to see me later that afternoon.

*Good, I plan to ask him when I will get out of here and go home.*

*Pause. Breathe.*

Around noon I heard what sounded like a hospital bed coming down the hall. Indeed it was. *Yay!* My mom was coming. I was feeling happy to see her. I smiled and attempted to straighten myself.

## ♫ "Happy" (Pharrell Williams) ♫

Just returning from surgery, she was still groggy from the anesthesia. We were both secured to our own beds, so I could not even reach her. Surely when she fully woke up, I would get the greeting I'd expected.

## 16 | INTERROGATED

Well, not exactly… in fact, it felt more like an interrogation.

Please know my mom is usually super-sweet, calm, and supportive. In that moment, however, she was rather curt. She began by just uttering my name.

"Cheri!"

As soon as I heard her tone, confusion set in. I had heard this tone before when she was irritated and scolding me for something. *Was I in trouble? What in the world could I have done?*

She continues, "After we were run over, when we were on the ground, in the snow, did you hear me calling for you?!"

*And there it is.*

Feeling the heat rise to my face and avoiding eye contact, *I said, "Um, I heard you."* Then, stumbling over my words, I explained that I'd asked the older gentleman with the crystal-blue eyes and plaid flannel shirt to tell her I was fine.

"I never saw a man with a flannel shirt and eyes like that," she said sharply. "No one told me anything."

"Mom, I'm so sorry," I said, but I was thinking, *Why I have been looking forward to this reunion for two days? So much for my mom being happy to see me.*

I thought of the man with the same crystal blue eyes, just like my Granny Wade. He had stayed with me just long enough to keep me calm at a time when I felt so very alone. Now I questioned whether he'd been real or just my imagination. Either way, I am thankful he appeared in my life. He was there for me, by my side, exactly when I needed him. There for a reason.

# Chapter Seventeen
# Shattered

During our hospital stay, my surgeon, Dr. Byrd, made quite an impression on me. He had a quiet confidence and moseyed into our room in his white lab coat with pens in the outer pockets and a stethoscope around his neck. In some strange way, he reminded me of John Wayne.

Though he was an older gentleman, I could see he was a good-looking man. Crow's feet accented his blue eyes. The lines on his face were distinguished. He had life experience. I felt I could trust this man and his expertise as a surgeon. He was all business when he spoke to me and Mom about our surgeries and healing processes. Then, at some point, the conversation turned to his interest in horses. That's when we could see the twinkle in those baby-blue eyes and the conservative, crooked smile that lit up his face.

In my mind, I imagined him pulling onto the horse track property and kicking up dust, driving a powder blue Mercedes two-door sedan. He likely dressed in a classy style outside the hospital. He probably wore a suit or maybe tan pleated dress pants that were cuffed with a fedora resting on his head to lessen his squint on sunny days.

Funky patterned dress socks surely accented his brown laced dress shoes. Whatever he actually wore at the track, I am confident that a whisper and a bit of celebrity status followed him. No doubt, ladies would peek over their shades, smile, and giggle as he passed by, attempting to capture his attention. And, being the gentleman he was, he would likely respond with a wink, a nod, and a tip of his hat.

I enjoyed asking questions and hearing his stories about his horses. After all, we were there long enough. It was enjoyable to learn about his passion outside of medicine. The twinkle in his eye was all about the magnificent thoroughbreds. During his rounds, he would marvel at the length of my femur bone. "You know, your femur bone is the longest I've ever seen on a human! You have a femur bone like a thoroughbred!"

I'm sure he meant that in the most complimentary way, but when you're eighteen and being compared to a horse…? I just could not share his enthusiasm.

"In fact," he continued, "I got a rod in there during your surgery, and it just was not long enough, so I had to take that rod out and get an even longer one!"

He must have shared this story a dozen times during our long hospital stay.

He went on to report that during my surgery, he actually placed the middle part of my bone on the surgery table and then wired it back in place. They opened me up, inserted the rod through my hip, wired my bone back in place, then stapled me up. The tender scars on my body remain as a reminder.

Mom and I would actually look forward to our interactions with Dr. Byrd. He was interesting and well-respected. One day he asked me about my plans for college, my future career. I told him that I was planning to be a physical therapist in the schools, proudly adding that I already had my first shadowing experience following my first semester of college. My plans were in motion. I was even looking forward to participating in my own healing with the physical therapists at the hospital. I saw it as my second unexpected field experience.

Hearing this, Dr. Byrd's brows scrunched into a scowl. "Physical therapy?" he scoffed, "Oh, no, you don't want to do that! You need to be a doctor!"

I continued to share my feelings, saying I was looking forward to working with physical therapists at the hospital, as that would help me to be productive while I was there. I adjusted my mindset to view this as a field experience and an opportunity to learn. I was ready "to be the patient."

"Oh, nooooo," he responded. "You don't need physical therapy. I fixed you."

Initially, I thought he was kidding, but then he added, "I'm not ordering physical therapy."

*What? Not ordering physical therapy? You must be kidding me. My leg is broken.* I was already planning to get the inside scoop on the life of a physical therapist working in the hospital. My plan, my checklist, was modified for the hospital field experience as the patient. Then, in one conversation, my plan had crumbled yet again. *I'm alone in my thoughts. Now what?*

*Pause. Breathe.*

There were blessings during our long hospital stay. Mom and I transitioned from a traditional mother-daughter relationship to a friendship. This was a new depth in our connection that was never to be broken. Together, we would experience life's heartbreaks and disappointments in the hospital as well as celebrate the small wins – mostly hers. All I could do was lay there, stuck on my back, attached to my bed, and still in traction. My life was on pause, the opposite of my usual always-on-the-go schedule.

We came to know our caring nurses and look forward to their shifts at the hospital. "When will you be here next?" we frequently asked Carla.

After all, no one stayed on the eighth floor for more than a few days. The labor and delivery nurses were so very sweet at City Hospital in Martinsburg, West Virginia, and Mom and I needed to be in the presence of these warm, caring, smiling faces. Carla and a couple of others kept our room cheerful, adding decorations and opening the curtains to let the light shine in.

We were stuck in our beds at the end of the hall; however, occasionally, as a special treat, our nurses would hold the newborn babies in the hallway so we could get a glimpse. It was a gift of hope, seeing new life. The sweet little babies were just what we needed to lift our spirits. It was proof that life existed outside of our room on the eighth floor.

Mom also shared her heartbreak over losing a baby boy before I was born. When I told her I'd always wanted an older brother, I got a surprising response: "Cheri, I'm just not sure we would have had more kids had your older brother survived."

*Everything works out for a reason. I'd never considered that not being born was a possibility.*

"Even if we still had you," she gently explained, "that would have been three children. That would have been it. Jon would not have been born." *I cannot imagine life without my younger brother.* She then added, "I always wished we had another boy, a brother for your brother."

## 17 | SHATTERED

While in the hospital, there was a "get real" sort of attention to life. I was accustomed to being an independent young lady; now there was an amount of helplessness, an admission that we were both vulnerable. I was forced to slow down — time for my body to heal. There were lessons to be learned; accepting help was humbling.

Later that month, I was on the phone with one of my besties, Leah. She worked in the business office at Fairmont State College.

"Cher," she said in a soft, sympathetic voice, "It is the last day to withdraw before you are marked as failing. I'm sorry. It's time."

Leah was right. I had to face the facts. Clearly, I would not be attending class this semester – I was not even out of bed! (Remember, this was 1990, and there was no such thing as online learning.)

Heartbroken and with tears streaming down my face, I withdrew from college. What about my plans?

*Pause. Breathe.*

In the following weeks, I remained in bed, still attached to the metal pulley system and unable to move. Mom, on the other hand, had been progressing well and was even walking again. One day, Dr. Byrd came into our room and smiled at her. "How would you like to go home?"

His back was to me, so he didn't see the scowl on my face as I listened to their discussion. Remember, the hospital was three hours away from home. *Wait, what? Release my mom? What about me? Why am I still attached to the bed?*

When I asked him, he turned to me and said casually, "Oh, no you're not ready. We need to keep you for at least two more weeks."

Complete panic washed over me. "No! I cannot stay here any longer," I pleaded as I did my best to sit up. "Please, please, please let me go too. I promise! I will do anything you say."

He said only that he would think about it, then he left our room. The following day the good doctor returned and announced that I had to do two things before I could get discharged. I was all ears.

"I will do anything to go home."

#1: I had to walk. (*Yes, please!*)

#2 I had to have a bowel movement. (Pun intended)

*Okay, got it. I have to walk, and I have to poop – not necessarily in that order.*

The reality is that I had done neither for the duration of my stay. I had been eating, so you think I would process some shit.

"Well, if you can't do it by yourself," Dr. Byrd said, "We can help."

The nurse came into the room (*Excuse me, you are putting that where?*), and just like that, I had my first enema. They informed me that it should not be long and to push the call button when I was ready for the bedpan. *Awkward!!*

As the nurse came into our room, she helped me prop myself up on the metal bedpan. My first reaction: *Brrr.* The bedpan was freezing cold! I was hanging onto the metal triangle, trying to hold myself up while my leg was still in traction and the bolt, pulley, and the weights still in place. In addition, my mom is in the room. The nurse is in the room. Here I am, the fashionista, trying to hoist myself up and balance while hanging onto the chain-linked metal triangle, relax, and poop.

Putting everything else out of my mind, I focused all my energy on the fact that this was my ticket home. What should have been a magical experience, the creamy poop of a mystic unicorn (or, like the squatty potty advertises: "The best poop of your life") instead sounded something like tink, tink. Tink, tink...

It was my hard little turds hitting the metal bedpan. *It sounded like Skittles coming out of my ass.* And yet... I had pooped! Check item #2 off the list.

The process for the number one task did not happen until the next morning. Dr. Byrd sauntered into the room with an extra spring in his step and a devilish grin. His arms were behind his back and clearly holding something. At my confused look, he smiled wider and showed me what appeared to be huge heavy-duty hedge clippers and an enormous crank of some sort.

Without much more than a "Good morning," he snipped off the left side of the bolt. I let out a startled gasp. *What are you doing?* Dr. Byrd then connected a crank to the bolt that my body had accepted as part of its own. I reached for my leg.

*Breathe, Cheri, just breathe.* The pressure continued to build as he tried to unscrew the threaded bolt out of my shin, but it was stuck. It would not budge. The pressure became so intense it felt like it might shatter my bone. *Please, stop!* It broke loose, only to be replaced with the strangest friction I'd ever felt – a hundred times worse than nails on a chalkboard. Once the metal bolt began to rotate, it kept catching on my bone.

*Wait, please! I need a minute. It is too much.*

The challenge of turning the crank was evident by the look on Dr. Byrd's face. The problem was the calcification around the bolt. It did not matter how much I pleaded for him to give me a break. He would only pause to collect the sweat off his brow with his sleeve.

On and on it went – the grinding, the continuous friction, more grinding. Imagine attempting to twist a metal rod held tightly in a vice… then it slips. The strange friction made me shiver all over. "There's nothing I can do for you," Dr. Byrd said, "It's bone pain." I held my breath and gripped tightly onto the metal bars of my hospital bed that had become an extension of me. I was cognizant that my mom was on the other side of the room, having to hear this strange agony.

Suddenly, he was still. The bolt was out. I felt relieved.

Walking for the first time since the accident was a joy. My nurses could see my height. "Oh my, you're so tall." I get butterflies in my belly and smile from ear to ear as I walk again. After lying down for so long, I feel the pull of gravity on my body, like a small child is holding onto me. With assistance from the therapists, crutches, and a titanium rod in the middle of my bone, I walked. I was walking for the first time since that snowy January 8th. *I was determined. And one day, I would run. And I would dance again.* I felt determined to resume my life. Suddenly, I was aware of time. The time that was lost here in the hospital. I was ready for my escape. Tomorrow my dad would be back to take us home.

*Pause. Breathe.*

## ♪ "Freedom" (George Michael) ♪

# Chapter Eighteen
## Escape

*Today is the day. It feels so strange to be leaving this place.* The hospital had been my home for a season. Mom and I were wheeled out the doors at the front of the hospital. *Is this really necessary?* Mom was loaded into the front passenger seat of our car; then, with a little maneuvering, I was stretched across the backseat. Having such long legs – the right one in a stiff brace that did not bend – left me not an inch to spare.

Dad slid into the driver's seat, and off we went. It was chilly outside, and the roads were clear. I peered out the window, filled with gratitude that our unexpected stay in Martinsburg, West Virginia, had come to an end.

> *I am thankful to the doctors and nurses who helped us. I am thankful that the hospital was full and we had the opportunity to meet the labor and delivery nurses and stay on floor eight. It was just meant to be. I will always remember the nurses fondly – for a reason and for a season.*

My mind played tricks on me several times during our ride home. I would startle and would insist that my dad slow down. I would make wild death grips on the back of Mom's seat at random moments, experiencing the sensation of sliding. The overwhelming feeling of being out of control on that day in January forever changed the course of my life.

The next few months would be filled with challenges. My relationship with my boyfriend would soon end. Jeff was my boyfriend for merely a season. Feeling an unexplainable urge to live life, I worked hard at home in charge of myself and my own therapy. I desired to get well and to once again be able to trust my body. I was determined to get better and live life.

After all, I could have died, probably should have died, and the fact that I didn't means I was meant to be here. *But what about my plans?* Remember, my original thought was that I would have physical therapy, regain my strength, and learn from the process in a way that would assist me in my future career. But, wait, my plan had fallen apart. There were no physical therapy orders. No college classes, no boyfriend, no social life.

*What now? I must create a new plan.*

## ♪ "Break My Stride" (Matthew Wilder) ♪

I knew that in order for things to change, I had to take ACTION. I had to become my own advocate. Over the next several months, I worked on myself both mentally and physically. I made the decision. *I can!*

No one was going to tell me otherwise. It was my decision. My stubborn streak kicked in. After all, my zodiac sign is Taurus, the bull. I decided I needed to stay connected to my friends. And that was just what I was going to do.

I started moving more and more. I did not just wear sweatpants and t-shirts and lay around. I started to get dressed, really get dressed. I was not disappointed if no one was going to see me and my outfit; I saw myself. I did it for myself, unlike that brunch in January when I wanted to be seen by others. I did my own physical therapy exercises. I showered. I got dressed, put on my make-up, and fixed my hair like I was ready to go out. I was determined to make new plans. Eventually, I convinced my parents that it was time. I must get out of the house.

My motivation was to return to college. I had an intense FOMO (Fear of Missing Out) happening. Next, I argued that it was no problem for me to drive, even though my right leg – my driving leg – was still in a non-bending brace. It was going to take some creativity to prove that I could handle myself. I would be driving a small, blue two-toned Toyota Corolla. Showing up to events was strange in the beginning, with my leg in a brace and my hands clamped onto crutches. Some friends showed concern: "Watch the leg!" *Somehow, I wasn't too concerned. I needed a social life. I would drive, and I would dance.*

When I drove, I put my crutches in the backseat, my right leg on the dashboard by the front window sill. I drove with my left foot. No big deal, right? I thought I was pretty slick. Then, while driving home late one night after being out at the club with my sorority sisters, I saw the flashing lights and the orange cones.

*Oh no!* It was a sobriety checkpoint. Were there rules about driving with your left foot? I had the EMT's and policeman's attention for a moment. *I'm sure they had never had someone through their checkpoint quite like me. I feel like the circus sideshow.* "Hey Frankie, come look at this." Here we go. I am grateful they allowed me to pass through without the hassle of getting out of the car. *I was determined. I can drive. I can socialize.*

Being involved in sorority life, and sponsoring my little sister, Lori Provenzano, was huge. Lori was such a doll and helped me feel like I belonged when I most needed it. You never know the difference you can make in someone's life just by being kind. I am forever grateful to my sorority sisters for permitting me to get back into the swing of things.

## ♫ "Back to Life" (Soul II Soul) ♫

Returning to school in the fall – and attempting to formulate a new plan – was challenging. I would change my major a couple more times before deciding to pursue a Bachelor of Arts degree in Elementary Education. Also, because I was a semester behind, I missed graduation with my pledge sisters. They would move on, and many of us lost touch with each other. And I missed my man. Scott and I were together by that time, but he had graduated and moved to Ohio for a job. *Pause. Breathe.*

## ♫ "I Just Called to Say I Love You" ♫
## (Stevie Wonder)

# Chapter Nineteen
## *Action*

I was no stranger to feeling alone. I had felt that way after the accident; when my pledge sisters graduated from college; when Scott moved back to Ohio for his job; and after the loss of my parents. Now I was experiencing the loss of my career and the loneliness of MS. *Where do I belong? What is my purpose? After twenty-five years as an educator, now what would I do with myself?*

♫ **"Alone" (Heart)** ♫

Then, traveling back in time to 1963, I thought, *What if my dad had sorted his laundry properly? Would a connection at the laundromat have occurred? Would I even exist? Maybe it's all part of the plan. Did my life happen for a reason? Is life a choice?*

My vision board still hangs in my room for daily reflection:

- Going Places
- Always Be Kind
- Eat Well, FEEL Great
- Dream Big
- Choose Your Powerful
- IGNITE BRILLIANCE
- You Got This!

### ♫ "Don't Stop Believin'" (Journey) ♫

Focus on my words. Let your mind travel as you imagine yourself five years from now. What do you want your life to look like, beginning with the moment you wake to start a new day? In your mind, look around the room. Let go of limiting beliefs. Really believe that anything is possible. What do you see? Feel it. Embrace it.

Where do you reside? An apartment? House? Condo? Think of the location. Your environment. Are you traveling? Working? Vacationing? How is the weather? Warm and sunny, or cold and snowy? Imagine your closet and getting dressed for your day. What clothes are you wearing? Uniform? Scrubs? Suit? Vacation attire? Picture the details in your mind. Pause.

Are you embarking on a new career? Are you retired? A new hobby? A new adventure? What would your life look like? How does it feel?

Are you willing to be brave? Who is with you? Pay special attention to relationships, those that make you feel good and raise your energy. Surround yourself with those who support, encourage, and empower you. Do you have meaningful quotes that inspire you in a visible place?

Do you believe in the Law of Attraction? That we attract certain people into our lives? Do we cross paths with others to teach us lessons? I have met so many amazing people that it feels like a cliché to categorize them as "for a reason, a season, or a lifetime."

### ♫ It's My Life" (Bon Jovi) ♫

As I reflected on my life over the past few years, I worried that I had given up by accepting help. Accepting help feels humbling; it's like admitting that I agree that "I can't." I'm trying to find a balance that

# 19 | ACTION

is acceptable to me where I still feel worthy. I need to feel that my life is still meaningful.

I've found inspiration and solace in the words of visionaries like Clara Barton, who said, "She remembered who she was, and the game changed." These words resonate; they remind me that there is still a fire burning in my belly. I'm not ready to be a spectator; I have more to contribute to the world. I choose to be relevant. I want to be seen. I am also exhilarated by Teddy Roosevelt's speech, "The Man in the Arena," which was shared by Brené Brown in her Netflix Special, *The Call to Courage*, and in her book, *Daring Greatly*.

> *It's not the critic who counts; not the man who points out how the strong man stumbles or where the doer of deeds could have done them better. The credit belongs to the man who is actually in the arena, whose face is marred by dust and sweat and blood; Who strives valiantly; Who errs, who comes short again and again, because there is no effort without error and shortcoming; but who does actually strive to do the deeds; who knows great enthusiasm, the great devotions; who spends himself in a worthy cause; who at the best knowns in the end the triumph of high achievement, and who at the worst, if he fails, at least he fails while daring greatly so that his place shall never be with those cold and timid souls who know neither victory nor defeat.*

Delivered in 1910, Roosevelt's words reach out across time, vibrating in my soul and activating my urgency to share my story. It flows in a forceful way, though at times, it is challenging for my fingers to type the words as rapidly as they need to be written.

*Powered by the Pivot* is unlocking the chains that have held me down in life – those feelings of "I can't." After the accident, it was, "I can't walk"; "I can't leave the hospital"; "I can't attend college for a semester." Now, the physical limitations imposed on my body by MS cause daily frustrations. I don't like to think of them as holding me down. I don't want to say "I can't"; instead, what I will say is, "I am figuring out my physical limitations in a different way." I feel an intense desire to *show up* in the world. I am an MS Warrior. I may navigate my life differently, but I am still focused on my dreams. In my own special way, I will make a difference in our world. My life is a choice. I can choose to accept my disability, and I can also choose to Pause, to Breathe, and to Pivot. *Feeling broken* has been a theme in my life, but one I am releasing.

As Landon T. Smith states in *Meet Maslow,* "The first step in the road to self-actualization is what Maslow referred to as Metacognition." Smith continues, "It means that since you know there is something missing in your life, you have the ability to work on it." Initially, after my career ended, I felt a tremendous loss. My needs were not being met. My lack of belongingness and loss of belief in my abilities impacted my capacity for joy. I kept searching. I embraced and relived past hurts and listened to my gut, revealing thankfulness for all my experiences. As Mark Manson shares in his thought-provoking book, *The Subtle Art of Not Giving a F\*ck,* "The more I peer into the darkness, the brighter life gets."

The willingness to uncover and face my issues in my subconscious ignites my passion to embark on this writing journey – one I liken to the gestation period of pregnancy. I am grateful for the laughter and the joy of reliving vivid memories of childhood, as well as for discovering peace in the tearful moments of pause. Today, I am the proud parent of *Powered by the Pivot.* Thank you for your empathy as I share my story, my precious baby with you. I hope it helps you feel as marvelous reading it as I have felt writing it. (For my Color Street friends, I hope you "Feel Marbelous." Feeling Marbelous is my first full set of Color Street's dry nail polish that I wore in 2020.)

> **"Everything is unfolding in perfect timing. I trust. I believe. I receive."**

Believing I can live my purpose has made my challenges easier to face. In 2021, I painted a pink flower in remembrance of my mother, who I've been missing since 2002, with the drop of dew falling from the flower's petal representing my teardrop. My most fervent hope in telling my story is that I honor my lovely mother, Barbara Wade Warcholak, with every word.

*Powered by the Pivot* is my self-actualization of Maslow's Hierarchy, the Pyramid of Needs, the peak, and my purpose. My involvement with Color Street as a stylist, the belongingness I feel by using the Alinker, being open about my struggles, and living life as an MS warrior, have all helped play a pivotal role in the needs that went unfulfilled after leaving the world of education.

## ♫ "Unwritten" (Natasha Bedingfield) ♫

Are you ready to face the shadows, your fears? Will you choose to be brave, feel empowered, and take action? Be gentle with yourself as you choose your own path to "Shake the World." Just like a flower needs sunlight, air, and water, our needs must be met, and our souls must be nurtured to grow. Nourish the beauty in you to experience wellness.

Envision the life you wish to create and do it because you "feel" it, you desire to learn more, and it brings you joy. Marianne Williamson says it brilliantly: "Do what makes your heart sing." I am thankful for so many experiences that have made my heart sing, including sharing my journey through writing. My life is meaningful and, some might say, serendipitous.

I hope my story inspires your journey to self-actualization. Believe in yourself. Find your Solitude. Pause, Breathe, and Pivot; Manifest Peace, Love, and Gratitude. "Choose your Powerful." And Bloom.

# Epilogue

**March 30, 2023**

My life feels like the situation when my bracelet broke on travel day. I was in line at the airport for curbside check-in. As my son was helping me with my backpack to get my arm through the strap, my gemstone "protection" bracelet caught on the strap and broke. I stopped and watched as the beads bounced all over the concrete sidewalk in so many different directions. My heart sank. Why now? My son, seeing the *Oh no!* expression on my face, said simply, "Mom, it did its job." I PAUSE, speechless, and think about my gemstone bracelet. Although I did enjoy wearing it, he was right, it was time to let it go.

While traveling to visit my daughter using the Alinker walking bike, I once again felt belongingness in the airport. Being able to walk with my Alinker meant feeling included by keeping up with everyone. This simple experience provided me with tremendous joy. I was surely walking with my Alinker smiling from ear to ear. I recognize that walking through a crowded airport may have annoyed me in the past. Now I am so lucky that I feel tremendous joy from simply strolling through the airport with a crowd and being at eye level. I'm feeling more confident about facing the world and greeting other people. I am so fortunate to experience joy from what most feel like a task of getting from point A to point B. Feeling seen was a delightful experience. I can BREATHE again.

### ♫ "Broken & Beautiful" (Kelly Clarkson) ♫

As I consider the notion that parts of my life had to be broken in order to fully appreciate them, my mindset shifts. Do we take time for gratitude and appreciate the small things in life? I think about the lessons my daughter learned throughout her childhood by watching my progression of MS. She learned lessons of appreciation for even the smallest moments. She inspires me to reflect on certain chapters of my life with gratitude. *Time to PIVOT and appreciate the lessons.*

## ♫ "All I Want" ♫
## (Teenear feat. Brandon Gomes)

The return of my independence to go where I wanted to go because I wanted to go was freeing; I was no longer "chained" to a transport chair. I reflect on my challenges: my broken bones from the car accident, the feeling like I was drowning in the emotion from my MS diagnosis, and I realize that it is only due to being broken that I am able to live this beautiful life. I have been meeting only the kindest people, who are the people I am meant to meet; I have made so many fortuitous connections of my own. I tell my husband, who worries about me traveling by myself, "It's okay; I'm a "Kindness Magnet." My life, although filled with challenges, is a privilege. I feel lucky to have met so many wonderful people and learned so many lessons by experiencing and reflecting on those challenges.

Take time to reflect on your own lessons in life. We all have obstacles to face. Is it time to embrace your own challenges? Will you choose to *PAUSE*, to *BREATHE*, and to *PIVOT*?

My hope is for you to feel *"Powered by the Pivot."*

# About the Author

Cheri Warcholak Lohrey was born in Virginia and raised in West Virginia, with strong ties to Florida. In 1990, Cheri's life was forever altered when she, along with her mother and sister, were struck by what she refers to as a "metal beast" of an automobile. This was when she made the first conscious decision to "pivot" so she would not only survive, but thrive.

Four years later, Cheri married her college sweetheart, Scott, and they moved to Ohio where they raised two children and fur babies. After twenty-five years of service as an educator- teacher, and middle school counselor, Cheri and her family decided to pivot toward a climate that would better accommodate her multiple sclerosis. Thus began their new journey in Nevada.

In life and through her writing, Cheri approaches the heavy moments, from the accident to the dark days after the MS diagnosis, with humor and gratitude. Her intention is to empower others with her "never give up" attitude; her hope is that the book will ignite their desire to Pause, to Breathe, and to Pivot. *Powered by the Pivot* is Cheri's first published book.

## Stay Connected

Website: cherilohrey.com

Facebook: Cheri Warcholak Lohrey

Instagram: @PoweredbythePivot Cheri Warcholak Lohrey

## Color Street:

colorstreet.com

NoMoreGnarlyNails.com

colorstreet.com/cheri22

colorstreet.com/incomedisclosure

## On the Cover - Cheri wore:

- Color Street's Cheeky Products

- Superstar - Highlighter Balm; Celebrity & Dreamer Powder Highlighter

- Go Getter - Blush Balm; Bashful & Diva Powder Blush

- Fearless - Bronzer Balm; Posh & Savvy - Powder Bronzer

- VIP- lipstick

- "Social Butterfly" - Glitter, dry nail polish.

- T. Jazelle bracelet from White's Fine Jewelry, Fairmont WV

*Need a Stylist: Go to colorstreet.com and enter your zip code to connect with a Color Street Stylist near you.*

*In my opinion, these products are Fun, Fashionable, & Fabulous!*

## My Favorite Tarte Products:

- Shape Tape, Cloud coverage (light-med neutral)
- Shape Tape, Ultra Creamy Concealer (29N, light medium)
- Tarte, Sugar Rush, Sweet Cravings- eyeshadow palette

## On the back:
CAbi- Cheri wore the Pose Jacket; spring 2022 collection.

## Are We Already Connected?

MS Warrior

Alinker Family

Color Street Stylist- Team YOUnited

## School Counselor:

Riverside Local Schools, Painesville Twp., Ohio

South Euclid - Lyndhurst City Schools, Lyndhurst, Ohio

## Teacher:

Painesville City Schools, Painesville, Ohio

**Fitness Instructor:**

Central YMCA, Painesville, Ohio

**Graduate School:**

Kent State University, Kent Ohio

**Undergraduate Degree:**

Fairmont State University (formerly Fairmont State College)

Fairmont, West Virginia

Sigma Sigma Sigma National Sorority

**High School:**

Fairmont Senior High School, Fairmont, West Virginia

**Grade Schools:**

Fairmont Catholic Grade School (Grades 1-8), Fairmont, WV

White Hall Elementary School (kindergarten)

# Acknowledgments

The spark to write this memoir was ignited by so many people I love. Thank you for believing in me before I believed in myself, and for encouraging me to write and share my story.

To Leah Woodburn, true friend of my heart; to my aunt, Sharon Wade Kisner – you are an amazing woman and a role model of a life well lived. To Heather Moran and Jen McCann, thank you for your unwavering support and sisterhood. Now is the right time. I'm an open book.

My life has been influenced so greatly by my parents and my grandparents. My mom, Barbara Wade Warcholak, always said, "You live, and you learn," and indeed, the lessons I learned through my challenges have made me who I am today. Thank you, Mom, for your gentle influence. I wholeheartedly miss you and dedicate my book to you.

Thank you to my husband, Scott, who knows, loves, and supports me like no other. You are my soulmate, an incredible gift in my life, and the man I wished for years before I even knew you existed.

Thank you to my son, Alex, who listened to my voice and reminded me that my counseling skills do make a difference. I am so proud of your drive to discover what lies beyond and your honorable service to our country. To my daughter, Aryn – you illuminate joy in life; your spirit and determination are remarkable. Thank you for sharing your authentic self, for our incredibly strong bond, and your deep-rooted connection to my soul. You brightened my life at the perfect time when I was mourning the relationship with my own mother. I'm honored to be your mom and so very proud of you.

To Christine Creviston and Sue Montgomery, my longtime friends – you are caring and patient beyond words. Thank you for being so attentive, supportive, and sympathetic when I shared my raw, unedited journey with you. I'm so very grateful for you both.

Thank you to the Wade and Warcholak families. To Beth Warcholak Lyons, my dear sister, who was part of the Pivot, who fills in the gaps and understands that day like no one else on earth. To my talented brother, Jon Warcholak – I love our "Mom talks." The depth of our connection that reaches the core, our sibling bond keeps the memories alive. To Janet and George, for being such a lovely part of my life. To Sharon Wade Kisner and Alyson Kisner Sarsfield, who visit to hear my voice, and for sharing special memories of our family that make us giggle and cause us to shed a few tears. Thank you to Uncle Anthony – though you have passed, your passion for ancestry continues to influence my life.

To Steffen and Lindsay Schmauss – we may not be related by blood, but you are family. I hold our sibling bond close to my heart. As Aryn says, "We could not have "chosen" a more perfect brother for Uncle Jon."

To the Lohrey family, especially my mother-in-law, Patricia Lohrey, who knows my story, yet still gets excited to read, listen and share the manuscript.

To my "sister" friends who encourage me to follow my heart and listen to my soul, thank you. To my lifelong bestie, Kim Branham Wilson, who knows exactly what to say when I need a kick in the pants, a good laugh, or an ugly cry.

To my two favorite high school teachers at Fairmont Senior High School: Mrs. Diana Munza, whose cheerful demeanor and teaching methods inspired an eagerness to do better and reach for greatness. You made learning enjoyable. And to Mrs. Linda Morgan, your presence

ACKNOWLEDGMENTS

upon entering the classroom caused me to sit a little straighter and lean in to hear your every word. I admire your eloquent style and your captivating lessons. You have influenced my life, always a role model of fashionable class. Thank you.

Thank you to my dear forever friend, Lisa Neroda, for the thought-provoking ideas of headlines. To Kelly Murphy, for your sound advice, friendship, and encouragement and for being "Kelly calm" in my life. To Nancy Archacki, my precious friend and future tour guide. To Lisa Artino, Kris Durkin, Tabitha Fuchs; to friends in Florida, West Virginia, or Ohio; friends in Mesquite or in Las Vegas – thank you for listening to me use *my voice* and share *my journey*.

To those of you who listened to my story before it went public, you know you are special to me. To friends from childhood and various "*I can*" chapters in my life that bring me so much joy. For those who reconnected after decades and chatted like we were together last month. Thank you. To Dan Whitely, for your artist inspiration and friendship. Whether you have been part of my life for a reason, a season, or a lifetime, I cherish you all.

Thank you to our "Weekend Family" at the lake – Dr. Kim Hollensworth, Dr. John and Grace Dumot, and The Malmer Family. Thank you for welcoming our family as part of yours and for touching our lives with fun times – your kind and generous nature does not go unnoticed. We will always cherish memories with you all at the lake. Hugs until we meet again. (Idea: wine at Caymus Vineyards, Napa Valley, California.)

To Shanda Trofe, Founder and Head Project Manager of Transcendent Publishing. Thank you for your incredible patience and guidance in transforming my dream into a reality. For your fabulous insight and reassurance – for encouraging me to dig a little deeper and be more vulnerable, yet in a supportive way - priceless! I feel so fortunate to have connected with you for my first writer's journey. The advice, excitement, and expertise you bring to writers is amazing!

To Dana Micheli, my trusted editor. Thank you for your resourcefulness and eagerness to assist with my journey. For authentically caring and helping my voice be heard. Your work is incredibly valuable and selfless. You provide writers like me the confidence to share the most vulnerable parts of our lives. Thank you.

For Selma Blair and Christina Applegate, my fellow MS Warriors, your power and your strength moves me. Thank you for being real, being visible, and sharing your challenges. You inspire, pave the way, and touch the lives of so many with your advocacy and authenticity. With heartfelt peace, love, and gratitude from a fellow MS warrior and fan. (For my thirtieth birthday, my ONLY request was a date night with my hubby to see *The Sweetest Thing*, which to this day remains my all-time favorite movie.) You both are absolutely marvelous! Goals to kick off my shoes together with you one day.

To Brené Brown – your research on shame, your message of courage, your books, namely *Daring Greatly,* and your storytelling, have all inspired me to "step into the arena." Thank you for leading the way, being brave, and sharing your powerful, life-changing message.

To Rob Sperry for asking the questions. Your skills are powerful and helped me discover my why, the one that made me cry. Thank you.

To Lisa Bilyeu, for "Radical Confidence," your storytelling is delightful. It helped me in my reflection of myself. Part of my "Pivot" was changing my verbiage and my mindset from "If" to "When." My goals and mission give me butterflies, plaster a smile across my face and make me think, "*Hell, yes!*" Despite my challenges, I believe Why *not* me? I CAN too! My new "radical" belief in myself: Don't underestimate me. I will find a way. #determined Thank you, Lisa!

## ACKNOWLEDGMENTS

To Matthew McConaughey, your story, *Greenlights* is a must-listen that made the drive from Ohio to Nevada enjoyable. I put in my earbuds and enjoyed three days of your storytelling. "Alright, alright, alright! Greenlight!" Thank you for helping me to be seen and feel belonging in the world.

To Stephen King, for your memoir *"On Writing"* and the advice that spoke to me. The first write is writing with the door closed. The rewrite is writing with the door open. I am ready to be open and share *Powered by the Pivot* with the world.

Thank you to Fa Park for your "Never Give Up" belief in life and pursuit of your own dreams. You are brilliant! Thank you to my Color Street Family, especially Team YOUnited, for your leadership and support.

Thank you to the Alinker family, especially BE Alink, inventor of the Alinker. I am so very grateful for your life-changing invention. The Alinker is freedom; it opens our world to possibility. Thank you for helping us to be seen again and feel belongingness in the world.

Thank you, Eliza Schlesinger, for the laughter. My publisher, Shanda, delightfully suggested a reward for myself for completing my book. I knew exactly what my reward would be. (Scott and I purchased tickets to see Iliza Schlesinger, stand-up comedian, in Las Vegas March 2023.) I was fortunate to meet you and get a picture with you. I love your body-positive segment for women on your Netflix special: Iliza Schlesinger: Elder Millennial, 2018. Thank you for sharing a positive message in a hilarious way. @howtobeeffortless

To Lindsey Sadowski, NET Neuro Emotional Technique Practitioner, who helped me reveal past hurts stuck in my subconscious, breathe through the challenges, and inspire me to envision my future and dream big.

To Carrie Stewart, LISW-S LCSW, for "tapping" into my subconscious through EMDR; Eye-Movement Desensitization Reprocessing.

Thank you to all who have played a part in my life by sharing your story, your writings, your message, your product, and your input. I feel so much appreciation for each of you and your valuable contributions to my mindset, which led me to share my story. A heartfelt thank you for your role in helping me bloom, growing in my confidence leading me to share my very personal story, *Powered by the Pivot,* with the world.

# Appendix One: "Powered by the Pivot" *Playlist*

Akon. *Lonely*. 1 Jan. 2005, https://audio-ssl.itunes.apple.com/itunes-assets/AudioPreview125/v4/dd/be/17/ddbe1750-c3e8-d76c-8948-5eba09cf926c/mzaf_10833438796338809324.plus.aac.p.m4a.

Bareilles, Sara. *Once Upon Another Time*. 18 Oct. 2013, https://audio-ssl.itunes.apple.com/itunes-assets/AudioPreview115/v4/a3/14/86/a31486cc-7c65-cacc-ea83-2119f9d9b231/mzaf_1774037101415274297.plus.aac.p.m4a

Bedingfield, Natasha. *Unwritten*. 30 Apr. 2007, https://audio-ssl.itunes.apple.com/itunes-assets/AudioPreview126/v4/5b/ad/55/5bad55f8-b4ef-a4c9-a518-b71c0fa0820b/mzaf_11068346438306862078.plus.aac.p.m4a.

Brooks, Meredith. *Bitch*. 24 Apr. 1997, https://audio-ssl.itunes.apple.com/itunes-assets/AudioPreview122/v4/91/7b/c7/917bc79a-fd5e-3f38-cbd2-353f75b583de/mzaf_8787009900511087214.plus.aac.p.m4a.

Buckingham, Lindsey. *Trouble*. 24 Mar. 2008, https://audio-ssl.itunes.apple.com/itunes-assets/AudioPreview125/v4/47/58/25/47582513-43ce-6e50-e738-8c66d2b82ee6/mzaf_17931139830128193420.plus.aac.p.m4a.

Clarkson, Kelly. *Broken & Beautiful (From the Movie "UGLYDOLLS")*. 27 Mar. 2019, https://audio-ssl.itunes.apple.com/itunes-assets/AudioPreview122/v4/8e/ec/32/8eec3298-826c-6837-b31e01fc798e973c/mzaf_4924608277558911595.plus.aac.p.m4a.

Edition, New. *Can You Stand the Rain*. 20 June 1988, https://audio-ssl.itunes.apple.com/itunes-assets/AudioPreview125/v4/03/58/c7/0358c740-14ec-ee9e-d339-29348cc08968/mzaf_86282860528971297.plus.aac.p.m4a.

Factory, Music. *Things That Make You Go Hmmmm....* 13 Dec. 1990, https://audio-ssl.itunes.apple.com/itunes-assets/AudioPreview112/v4/36/8e/f7/368ef7f9-5eb8-d431-93c8-5182cefeed74/mzaf_14892405816840589152.plus.aac.p.m4a.

Grits. *Ooh Ahh (My Life Be Like)* [Feat. Tobymac]. 1 Jan. 2022. https://audio-ssl.itunes.apple.com/itunes-assets/AudioPreview112/v4/1c/3c/37/1c3c379e-4121-2596-f147-3f9d2394aac1/mzaf_14976000597374526501.plus.aac.p.m4a.

Halen, Van. *Jump*. 9 Jan. 1984, https://audio-ssl.itunes.apple.com/itunes-assets/AudioPreview125/v4/cc/2f/d0/cc2fd073-8d0c-4a7d-630c-64639fbb56e1/mzaf_15726260092255257970.plus.aac.p.m4a.

Hammer. *U Can't Touch This*. 13 Jan. 1990, https://audio-ssl.itunes.apple.com/itunes-assets/AudioPreview112/v4/c3/b3/ac/c3b3acfe-07a7-4b50-5788-875d133d97c7/mzaf_3158069395319174581.plus.aac.p.m4a.

Harris, Calvin. *Feels (Feat. Pharrell Williams, Katy Perry & Big Sean)*. 15 June 2017, https://audio-ssl.itunes.apple.com/itunes-assets/AudioPreview125/v4/62/51/dd/6251dd8d-5586-ffe5-7583-0f9721e0967f/mzaf_5799837564730209127.plus.aac.p.m4a.

# APPENDIX ONE: PLAYLIST

Heart. *Alone*. 16 May 1987, https://audio-ssl.itunes.apple.com/itunes-assets/AudioPreview115/v4/48/6c/2a/486c2a0b-1857-5653-64d1-d8719b1b9930/mzaf_14556555269457036172.plus.aac.p.m4a.

Hill, Faith. *Breathe*. 4 Oct. 1999, https://audio-ssl.itunes.apple.com/itunes-assets/AudioPreview125/v4/e4/a1/d3/e4a1d307-f7cf-9937-cb55-8c57ef948ef6/mzaf_7697740475593988722.plus.aac.p.m4a.

Ice, Vanilla. *Ice Ice Baby*. 2 July 1990, https://audio-ssl.itunes.apple.com/itunes-assets/AudioPreview122/v4/27/2c/1b/272c1b06-f9aa-07db-10ff-635f07efd490/mzaf_12430973061039676987.plus.aac.p.m4a.

John, Elton. *I'm Still Standing*. 23 May 1983, https://audio-ssl.itunes.apple.com/itunes-assets/AudioPreview122/v4/51/63/fb/5163fbbe-1d5e-b64c-5a72-162c97f5d3de/mzaf_10426288777977575041.plus.aac.p.m4a.

Jordan, Montell. *This Is How We Do It*. 6 Feb. 1995, https://audio-ssl.itunes.apple.com/itunes-assets/AudioPreview122/v4/9c/3d/e2/9c3de254-297e-fc5f-5d3e-94d783f89518/mzaf_7233349672150407153.plus.aac.p.m4a

Journey. *Don't Stop Believin'*. 3 June 1981, https://audio-ssl.itunes.apple.com/itunes-assets/AudioPreview125/v4/e4/6c/ad/e46cad13-317a-3074-8d0f-a41af0bb2437/mzaf_5207796602846861401.plus.aac.p.m4a

Jovi, Bon. *It's My Life*. 8 May 2001, https://audio-ssl.itunes.apple.com/itunes-assets/AudioPreview125/v4/cc/71/0c/cc710cf4-7992-1f91-3b7f-3110a5ed8b6a/mzaf_10666462243667860728.plus.aac.p.m4a.

Khan, Chaka. *I Feel for You*. 1 Aug. 1984, https://audio-ssl.itunes.apple.com/itunes-assets/AudioPreview122/v4/fe/58/73/fe58736b-7063-dedc-fe49-b0ccd769cb8d/mzaf_10897176363479422436.plus.aac.p.m4a.

---. *I'm Every Woman*. 12 Oct. 1978, https://audio-ssl.itunes.apple.com/itunes-assets/AudioPreview112/v4/15/61/c9/1561c92f-9025-6101-7a7d-cf6996dd9fed/mzaf_8426147093356562015.plus.aac.p.m4a.

---. *True Colors*. 25 Aug. 1986, https://audio-ssl.itunes.apple.com/itunes-assets/AudioPreview125/v4/2b/f1/c1/2bf1c157-000b-8b87-a01b-3f1924d907dc/mzaf_4766252712161317129.plus.aac.p.m4a.

In-text Citation: (Lauper, *Girls Just Want to Have Fun*)

Lizzo. *About Damn Time*. 14 Apr. 2022, https://audio-ssl.itunes.apple.com/itunes-assets/AudioPreview112/v4/f2/9a/5f/f29a5f56-4409-75c5-9c87-5552a31dec7b/mzaf_2061585353109259019.plus.aac.p.m4a.

Kross, Kris. *Jump*. 31 Mar. 1992, https://audio-ssl.itunes.apple.com/itunes-assets/AudioPreview115/v4/ab/d2/d8/abd2d882-24c4-32e0-cf62-6fd907712284/mzaf_14473309192039866164.plus.aac.p.m4a.

Mario. *Just a Friend 2002*. 1 Feb. 2002, https://audio-ssl.itunes.apple.com/itunes-assets/AudioPreview115/v4/e6/96/d7/e696d794-4689-5e19-2e1b-6da2d975e13d/mzaf_1696735432894731506.plus.aac.p.m4a.

# APPENDIX ONE: PLAYLIST

McKnight, Brian. *Anytime.* 23 Sept. 1997, https://audio-ssl.itunes.apple.com/itunes-assets/AudioPreview115/v4/58/4e/28/584e2864-9aa4-a32e-829e-f61469a82b1c/mzaf_1246064508667893335.plus.aac.p.m4a

Michael, George. *Freedom! '90.* 3 Sept. 1990, https://audio-ssl.itunes.apple.com/itunes-assets/AudioPreview112/v4/b2/17/d2/b217d261-fcb6-f9b9-9762-6e6565934ee4/mzaf_12298286314066236474.plus.aac.p.m4a.

Miller, Jake. *Dazed and Confused (Feat. Travie McCoy).* 31 Oct. 2014, https://audio-ssl.itunes.apple.com/itunes-assets/AudioPreview112/v4/b7/1d/97/b71d9774-5886-1020-ce98-d85daef20b4c/mzaf_4386096516996155973.plus.aac.p.m4a.

Nature, Naughty By. *Hip Hop Hooray.* 10 Dec. 1992, https://audio-ssl.itunes.apple.com/itunes-assets/AudioPreview126/v4/69/4a/f7/694af710-dc43-fcd0-4d38-c065ad2c59b2/mzaf_2237244325260168591.plus.aac.p.m4a

Ocean, Billy. *Get Outta My Dreams, Get Into My Car.* 1 Jan. 1975, https://audio-ssl.itunes.apple.com/itunes-assets/AudioPreview115/v4/16/5a/8c/165a8c6b-ff8d-9421-9014-2df0c1fe8a1f/mzaf_13306663064027372766.plus.aac.p.m4a.

Paramore. *Hard Times.* 19 Apr. 2017, https://audio-ssl.itunes.apple.com/itunes-assets/AudioPreview115/v4/44/7c/ed/447cedf1-33e1-1c2b-d513-e2562f05a630/mzaf_3301205520917249272.plus.aac.p.m4a.

Paula, Paul &. *Hey Paula.* 28 Nov. 1963, https://audio-ssl.itunes.apple.com/itunes-assets/AudioPreview125/v4/aa/65/87/aa65873a-7b0d-1b37-dca0-015d180d91cf/mzaf_8469738787833633274.plus.aac.p.m4a.

Richie, Lionel. *Stuck On You*. 1 Jan. 1983, https://audio-ssl.itunes.apple.com/itunes-assets/AudioPreview122/v4/b2/e1/24/b2e1245a-f1aa-1627-c70a-fe39cdb20d3a/mzaf_3900009971421539217.plus.aac.p.m4a.

Rock, Rob Base &. DJ EZ. *Joy and Pain*. 9 Aug. 1988, https://audio-ssl.itunes.apple.com/itunes-assets/AudioPreview125/v4/39/b9/68/39b9687f-64c1-6c4f-c434-bb909c1b754f/mzaf_8236961169492288246.plus.aac.p.m4a.

Roots, Greg Street Presents Nappy. *Good Day (Feat. Nappy Roots)*. 1 Jan. 2008, https://audio-ssl.itunes.apple.com/itunes-assets/AudioPreview125/v4/41/7b/8d/417b8dcc-4bde-a5cc-436c-fb61716941bc/mzaf_11706371396836794141.plus.aac.p.m4a.

Sammy, Frank Sinatra &. *Me and My Shadow*. 1 Jan. 2014, https://audio-ssl.itunes.apple.com/itunes-assets/AudioPreview118/v4/16/07/c5/1607c55c-3dbf-94da-4572-add8bc053082/mzaf_2676944732266552024.plus.aac.p.m4a.

Soul, Soul II. *Back to Life*. 10 Apr. 1989, https://audio-ssl.itunes.apple.com/itunes-assets/AudioPreview125/v4/9f/4f/83/9f4f8399-88f8-edf9-d5e5-7865b06f8c0b/mzaf_5810987265422915618.plus.aac.p.m4a

Spearhead, Michael Franti &. *The Sound of Sunshine (Single Version)*. 1 June 2010, https://audio-ssl.itunes.apple.com/itunes-assets/AudioPreview115/v4/67/33/4e/67334e58-da1f-87ca-82a6-05565d72a689/mzaf_7252807199828930963.plus.aac.p.m4a.

Survivor. *Eye of the Tiger*. 29 May 1982, https://audio-ssl.itunes.apple.com/itunes-assets/AudioPreview112/v4/2d/f6/6e/2df66ed5-672a-cdc4-5938-4c0ef15f8ec4/mzaf_10078610458246320307.plus.aac.p.m4a

# APPENDIX ONE: PLAYLIST

Teenear. *All I Want (Feat. Brandon Gomes)*. 12 Dec. 2022, https://audio-ssl.itunes.apple.com/itunes-assets/AudioPreview112/v4/8f/49/00/8f490067-04cc-e1be-4be4-925e631baa0f/mzaf_13640827799610640323.plus.aac.p.m4a.

The Andrews Sisters. *I'll Be With You in Apple Blossom Time*. 3 Feb. 1990, https://audio-ssl.itunes.apple.com/itunes-assets/AudioPreview125/v4/b0/1a/82/b01a829e-7187-9faa-7710-d5cdb47b2ce9/mzaf_13308152542220723316.plus.aac.p.m4a.

The Pointer Sisters. *I'm So Excited*. 1 July 1982, https://audio-ssl.itunes.apple.com/itunes-assets/AudioPreview125/v4/34/7c/14/347c1412-5d9d-b7b4-67ed-8a06683135f2/mzaf_2588790863790002343.plus.aac.p.m4a.

Trainor, Meghan. *Mom (Feat. Kelli Trainor)*. 6 May 2016, https://audio-ssl.itunes.apple.com/itunes-assets/AudioPreview125/v4/05/d5/b8/05d5b837-9d11-5354-0334-a5d1657eb030/mzaf_3825830283484527872.plus.aac.p.m4a.

Underground, Digital. *Same Song*. 1 Jan. 1991, https://audio-ssl.itunes.apple.com/itunes-assets/AudioPreview122/v4/c3/0f/c9/c30fc95e-c057-7138-9ef6-0dd25b1d709d/mzaf_2708187884519761384.plus.aac.p.m4a.

Wailers, Bob Marley &. The. *Three Little Birds*. 3 June 1977, https://audio-ssl.itunes.apple.com/itunes-assets/AudioPreview122/v4/bb/c0/13/bbc0130a-700f-8f3d-ecef-00092e6f356d/mzaf_14981696650587386665.plus.aac.p.m4a.

Watley, Jody. *Real Love*. 1 Jan. 1989, https://audio-ssl.itunes.apple.com/itunes-assets/AudioPreview125/v4/b5/af/75/b5af752f-d272-21fd-624c-451dfbe60e21/mzaf_9031497260336175527.plus.aac.p.m4a

Wilder, Matthew. *Break My Stride.* 1 July 1983, https://audio-ssl.itunes.apple.com/itunes-assets/AudioPreview122/v4/d8/71/0e/d8710e34-134a-3932-dd98-4241a624b02f/mzaf_11701803193029833261.plus.aac.p.m4a.

Williams, Pharrell. *Happy.* 19 Sept. 2014, https://audio-ssl.itunes.apple.com/itunes-assets/AudioPreview115/v4/46/5b/82/465b82ee-f7b1-fd5d-366a-eb164d809cb6/mzaf_6521804329652378308.plus.aac.p.m4a

Willingness. Hurricane. 22 Feb. 2023, https://audio-ssl.itunes.apple.com/itunes-assets/AudioPreview126/v4/41/28/cf/4128cf93-b4d1-6a4f-79f6-70679fbf42cc/mzaf_8906908269590655829.plus.aac.p.m4a.

Withers, Bill. *Lean On Me.* 1 Jan. 1972, https://audio-ssl.itunes.apple.com/itunes-assets/AudioPreview125/v4/7d/09/dd/7d09dd12-5575-cbc9-0322-30b47ed71959/mzaf_4631604567913745424.plus.aac.p.m4a.

Wonder, Stevie. *I Just Called to Say I Love You.* 21 Oct. 2002, https://audio-ssl.itunes.apple.com/itunes-assets/AudioPreview115/v4/cc/fe/33/ccfe3311-7f1e-8526-6557-0fd4be7d9f2c/mzaf_11674085368529152358.plus.aac.p.m4a.

Yanks, Frank Yankovic &. His. *Beer Barrel Polka.* 30 Aug. 1988, https://audio-ssl.itunes.apple.com/itunes-assets/AudioPreview115/v4/f0/f5/33/f0f5339d-5ad6-2840-8ae7-6efb51523b47/mzaf_15302273522351417244.plus.aac.p.m4a.

# Appendix Two: "Powered by the Pivot" Reading List

Iyeu, Lisa. *Radical Confidence*. Simon and Schuster, 2022.

Brown, Brené. *Daring Greatly*. Penguin, 2015.

King, Stephen. *On Writing*. Hodder & Stoughton, 2012.

Kingsbury, Karen. *Let Me Hold You Longer*. Tyndale House Pub, 2014.

Manson, Mark. *The Subtle Art of Not Giving a F*ck*. HarperCollins, 2016.

McConaughey, Matthew. *Greenlights*. Clarkson Potter, 2021.

Nepo, Mark. *The Book of Awakening*. Conari Press, 2000.

Smith, Landon T. *Meet Maslow*. Createspace Independent Publishing Platform, 2017.

Sperry, Rob. *6 Figures and Beyond*. 2021.

# Appendix Three: "Powered by the Pivot" *Binge List*

*Disney's Snow White and the Seven Dwarfs: Still the Fairest of Them All.* Dir. Arends, Harry Arends. Perf. Angela Lansbury, Ken Anderson, Rudy Behlmer, Studio N/A, 2001.

*Brené Brown: The Call to Courage.* 2019.

"The Wait Out." *Seinfeld,* created by Larry David and Jerry Seinfeld, season 7, episode #133, West-Shapiro Productions and Castle Rock Entertainment, 1996. Starring Jerry Seinfeld and Julia Louis-Dreyfus.

*Death Becomes Her.* Dir. Robert Zemeckis. Perf. Bruce Willis, Meryl Streep, and Goldie Hawn. Dan Lund Films, 1992, N/A.

*Popeye.* Dir. Robert Altman, Studio N/A, 1980.

*The Great Outdoors.* Dir. Howard Deutch. Per. John Candy, Dan Akroyd, and Annette Benning, Studio N/A, 1988.

*Introducing, Selma Blair.* 2021.

*Jurassic World.* Dir. Colin Trevorrow. Per. Chris Pratt and Bryce Dallas Howard. Studio N/A, 2015.

*Indiana Jones and the Raiders of the Lost Ark.* Dir. by Steven Spielberg. Per. Harrison Ford and Karen Allen. Studio N/A, 1981.

*The Birds.* Dir. by Alfred Hitchcock. Per. Tippi Hedren, Rod Taylor, and Jessica Tandy. Studio, N/A. 1963

*My Cousin Vinny.* Dir. Jonathan Lynn. Per. Joe Pesci and Marisa Tomei. Studio N/A, 1992.

*The Sweetest Thing.* Dir. Roger Kumble. Per. Christina Applegate, Cameron Diaz and Selma Blair. Studio, N/A, 2002.

# Appendix Four: Slogans and Quotes of *Inspiration*

Nike Campaign "Just Do It"

"In a gentle way, you can shake the world." Mahatma Gandhi

"Either write something worth reading or do something worth writing." Ben Franklin

"My mission in life is not merely to survive but to thrive and to do so with some passion, some compassion, some humor and some style." Maya Angelou

"She remembered who she was, and the game changed." Clara Barton

"I am willing to believe that things will always workout, even when they don't feel like it." And "Everything is unfolding in perfect timing. I trust. I believe. I receive." (@Iam.affirmations) on Pinterest.

"Be STRONG enough to stand alone, SMART enough to know when you need help, and BRAVE enough to ask for it." Ziad K. Abelnoor

# Appendix Five: Additional *Resources*

Sadowski, Lindsey, ATC, NET, Neuro Emotional Technique Practitioner: Toadalpositivity.com Toadalpositivity@gmail.com

EMDR Eye Movement Desensitization Reprocessing Therapy: emdria.org

**Products:**
- Alinker
- Cabi- Carol Anderson by Invitaion
- The Squatty Potty
- Life Pro
- Healthwave Mat
- Jimmy Fallon's Ultimate Sac
- Juice Plus+
- The MS GYM- Trevor Wicken

**Places visited during Lohrey family vacations:**

Las Vegas
- The Hoover Dam and Lake Mead
- The Skywalk, West Rim of the Grand Canyon
- The Freemont Experience
- Slotzilla- zipline through downtown Las Vegas
- Red Rock National Conservation Area

Willow Beach, Arizona- kayaking, the Colorado River: Emerald Cave

The Westin, Seven Mile Beach, Grand Cayman
    Stingray City excursion with Red Sail Sports
    Macabuka Bar & Grill
    "Paradise" in Georgetown, lunch & snorkeling location
    Hell: Grand Cayman Islands
    The Turtle Farm; Grand Cayman
Duck Key, Marathon Florida, Key West, Fort Lauderdale
    Hawk's Cay Resort, Duck Key, Florida - The Dolphin Connection
    Sunset Grille, Marathon, Florida
    Southernmost Point Buoy, Key West, Florida
    The Butterfly Conservatory, Key West
    Banana Cafe' & Cre'perie

Kauai Hawaii
    Waimea Canyon
    Spouting Horn
    Brenneke's Deli near Po'ipu Beach
    Kipu Ranch Adventures- UTV tour
    Holo Holo Excursions- The Napali Coast & Niihau SUPER TOUR, snorkeling the Lehua Crater orr Niihau's North Shore
    Tropical Dreams- dessert
    The Original Red Dirt Shirts
Maui, Hawaii: Kapilua Villas; Kapalua Resort.
Breakfast at Charlie's in Pa'ia
The Road to Hana
    The Seven Pools
Ho'okipa Beach Park in Paia
    Hawaiian Green Sea Turtles
Pearl Factory, Hawaii's Original Pearl In The Oyster
Anniversary Black Pearl Necklace
Haleakla National Park
Big Beach in Wailea
Excursion to Discover Lan'ai – Trilogy IV Lahaina, HI

# Thoughts of an *Expectant Mother* In 1973:

"Your Mother, Labor of Love"

A tiny seed born from trust, who loved you first?
Your mother
Perplexed was she at your first flutter, deep inside it was,
Your mother
As you grew within her womb; nourished now, you begin to bloom.
In the mornings when she's so sick,
You now gain strength and begin to kick.
Your mother
Surrounded now by coats of white,
The pain apparent, her lip she bites.
Your mother
The room goes dark, she is alone,
Quiet now, with nary a moan.
Doors burst open to reveal
Her nurse and baby – is this real?
Forgotten are the pain and woes,
For she's too busy counting fingers and toes,
You are her world, she loves you so,
Your mother.

– Sharon Wade Kisner 4.25.23

# Lessons Learned from our "Leaping" Leo

**Leap, Lick & Love like Leo**
**RIP Leo 9.13.16 - 4.7.23**

Our family certainly misses our sweet poodle
who passed unexpectedly:

### Leo the Licker:

From the time he was a pup, Leo licked everything
including his infamous "air licking"

### Leo the Cuddler:

Our sweet poodle was a "spooner" and would nuzzle right next to you and rest his head right on your lap, your leg or close to your heart. He would often wrap himself next to or on his brother Cosmo.

We miss Leo so much and remember him lovingly, feeling thankful he was part of our family. We can all learn a little from Leo...

May our hearts leap with joy.

May we taste goodness enough to keep licking.

May we take time to express our love and cuddle like Leo.

*Rest in Peace, Leo.*

Pause • Breathe • Pivot

Enjoy your journey with
Peace, Love, & Gratitude.

CPSIA information can be obtained
at www.ICGtesting.com
Printed in the USA
JSHW011914160723
44860JS00002B/5

9 798988 514749